How to Build a Playwright in Three Acts

How to Build a Playwright in Three Acts

Rachel Bublitz

Edited by Maria McConville

Published in 2026 by Stage Partners
PO Box 4795
Stamford, CT 06907
www.yourstagepartners.com

ISBN: 979-8-89099-260-4

Printed in the United States of America
10 9 8 7 6 5 4 3 2 1

Questions? Contact us at info@yourstagepartners.com

For Alex, I couldn't ask for a better partner.

Also for Keegan, who was ready to take the world by storm. May her memory be a blessing.

Contents

Editor's Preface

We all have our people. The type of people that we are drawn to, that we want to emulate. My type is "playwright." World Builders. Wordsmiths. Creators of characters that reflect our truest selves. No wonder I work in play publishing! I get to interact with these extraordinary storytellers daily.

I am fascinated by the playwriting process. An idea appears to the writer—a phrase that echoes in their heart, an image, a nagging question—and then they disappear for a time with this nugget of possibility. The playwright reemerges from their solitude with pages that take performers, designers, and audiences on an adventure.

Where to begin? How do you take the idea floating around your head and flesh it out into a three-act play? I have gone on this journey a few times as a playwright myself, and, honestly, I found that once I was past the exciting idea phase, the next steps were unclear, and I needed to wrestle the play out of me.

Cue Rachel Bublitz!

Personally, I have had the great fortune of being a part of Rachel's writing process a few times. I have acted as a dramaturg for a play she was reworking—it was delightful to see her dive back into the world of that play and rearrange its form. I have pitched her ideas for plays and watched her embark on the mission with so many questions, only to return with beautiful answers.

When Rachel came to Stage Partners and said, "I have an idea for a book on playwriting," we were game to go on this journey with her. I must tell you, this was no small feat. I watched as Rachel wrote and rewrote and rewrote in order to find a way to share a process that was so personal to her. What inspired me throughout was Rachel's relentless attitude and eagerness to get back into the pages and give us something that she wished she had when she was a new playwright.

Rachel Bublitz dares us to put pen to paper right out of the gate with *How to Build a Playwright in Three Acts.* We are not simply readers of this book. The book demands that we have a pen in our hand while we are reading. We are encouraged to make a mess with all of the ideas we have. She gives us methods of organizing the chaos to form bits of dialogue, then scenes, and finally our play.

I imagine each of us coming back to this book over and over again with each new idea that we can't shake and just need to turn into a play. I envision readers filling their margins with notes, a highlighter at the ready to capture the pieces of inspiration that will keep them at it. I hope teachers will take the unique exercises and apply them in their own lessons.

What I love about what Rachel so generously, thoughtfully, and sometimes painstakingly articulates for us with this book is the unique and personal process of writing a play. There are thousands of entry points to the play you are trying to write. This book celebrates the writing craft. By bravely embarking on this journey, the adventurer (you, the reader) becomes more and more a playwright. In a time when one can outsource the writing process to a computer, Rachel celebrates the creative endeavor that makes us so beautifully human.

I am so thrilled for you to dive in. You are my people, and I am in awe of you already. Now, time to write!

—Maria McConville
Director of Education & Engagement
Stage Partners
November 2025

Prologue

Practicing an art, no matter how well or badly, is a way to make your soul grow, for heaven's sake. Sing in the shower. Dance to the radio. Tell stories. Write a poem to a friend, even a lousy poem. Do it as well as you possibly can. You will get an enormous reward. You will have created something.

—Kurt Vonnegut

Fair warning: I am going to ask you to write nonsense. I am going to give you silly prompts. In fact, I am going to encourage you to stop thinking altogether and embrace whatever falls out onto the page. In the pages that follow, I break down the elements of dramatic writing and divide them into three acts: *Act One: Building a Toolbox*, where I'll cover essential dramatic tools; *Act Two: Building a Play*, where I'll dissect essential dramatic elements; and *Act Three: Building a Playwright*, where I'll share what's essential to my own process, and you can discover what is essential to yours.

Creation of any kind can be hard, painful even, and writing is no exception. We have a clear-as-crystal vision of what we *want* to create in our head, but somehow it comes out all muddled as it snakes its way onto the page. The gap between what we want to create and what our finished creation looks like can feel insurmountable. But it doesn't have to feel that way. I want this book to be a path to discovering the joy of creation. Kurt Vonnegut talked about how much creation and creativity feeds our souls, and I absolutely agree. Writing with the aim to feed your soul instead of the aim to make something "good" will have you pulling out a lot less hair. It's a lower bar. Actually, it's no bar. And the best part? If you hate it, you can rewrite it.

After all, when we work on dramatic writing, we can't forget what that thing is called . . . a *PLAY*. So, let's play. Make yourself laugh. Let go and run laps inside your own imagination. Yes, this book is about elements and definitions and examples, but it's also about learning how to *play* around and have fun with writing.

So take out a pencil and stretch your hands. Time to write!

Act One
BUILDING A TOOLBOX

UNLEASH

I HAVE TWO DOGS WHO KNOW that we're headed to the dog park as soon as we take a particular freeway exit. Yelping, jumping, howls—flat-out pandemonium. Once we're out of the car, it takes all my strength to hold their leashes. When we're finally through the gate, I unhook their leashes, and they're off like a shot. Like they've never gotten to experience something so phenomenal before, even though we come to this park weekly. They run with such pure joy, you can't look at them without smiling. And that's what we're going to do for your inner writer: take them out and let them loose.

It might be hard to get your inner writer excited. Your inner writer might look back at you with large eyes, brimming with tears, at even the suggestion that they go off and play. It's hard to be set loose when you have no experience of it: you just don't know what to do with yourself. But never fear! You can build up the stamina of your inner writer and get them used to being set free. In this chapter, we're going to try out two strategies for **unleashing** the writer within.

BRAIN DRAIN

The first tool I use to unleash the writer in me is something I call **brain drain**. This is a modified version of Julia Cameron's morning pages exercise (from her fabulous book, *The Artist's Way*). We need to practice getting our minds out of the way when we write. I know that sounds odd, since you'd think brains need to be pretty heavily involved in writing, but our brains often house our inner critic, who loves to judge every word before it even hits the page. Allowing words to just fall out as they see fit is a skill that takes patience and practice. The more work you put in, the easier you'll find it to let go of how your writing should or shouldn't look, and let it come out how it is. You'll have time to fix it at some point; that's what rewriting is all about.

The other benefit of this exercise is that it helps us to let go of a lot of everyday things our minds just love to hold onto: the fun plans you have coming up this weekend, that annoying thing your friend said at lunch, the huge pile of laundry sitting on your bedroom floor. These thoughts often pop up and get in our way when we set out to write. Draining your brain will not only help you to stop dwelling on them, but will also give you practice releasing those thoughts when you write, which will make that eventual first draft all the easier to get out.

Writing Cue ❯❯

Get a notebook, loose paper, or your laptop ready. What should you write? Literally anything! And I do mean anything. You could write a grocery list, lyrics to your favorite song, complaints about how much you hate this exercise; it could even be the same word over and over and over. Don't let your pen or pencil or keyboard stop until the timer goes off. Do not worry about punctuation or spelling or if your handwriting is legible or even if you're making any sort of sense whatsoever. No one is going to read this. In fact, when you're done, you can burn or rip up what you just wrote. Dealer's choice! What you write for **brain drain** isn't important; what is important is the practice of letting anything and everything fall out onto the page.

- Get a timer ready for two minutes.
- Get your writing tools ready, whether they're a notebook and pen or it's a new document on your computer.
- Spelling and punctuation are not important.
- This should be something that no one else will read! **Brain drains** are not for sharing.
- When you are ready, start the timer. That's right, GO!
- Write down anything and everything!
- Don't stop until the timer sounds.

❮ Interval ❯

- Stop writing once the timer sounds!
- Stand, stretch, move, shake it out.
    - This is an important step that I'll ask you to do every time you write. It's hard to make ourselves do new things, and rewarding our bodies with stretches and other movement that feels good helps to trick our brains into enjoying it!
- How did that feel?
    - The harder the **brain drain** is, the more often it should be used!
        - Create a regular schedule.
        - Start with two minutes and build up slowly from there.
    - Easy breezy lemon squeezy?
        - Double your timer next time!

- Did anything surprise you?
- Use the **brain drain** before future exercises to clear the cobwebs before you get to work.

BRAINSTORMING

While the brain drain exercise helps to clear the cobwebs and let our writing flow, **brainstorming** encourages that flow of thought into a particular direction for inspiration. We'll talk more about this zeroing in, or prewriting, as I like to think of it, in Act Two.

Brainstorming is the most flexible of all the tools we'll go through, and it's helped me out of my toughest writing pickles. It's there for you when you're trying to come up with ideas, or when you need to get out of your head, or when you want to think ahead and grow a little garden of ideas for yourself for future harvesting.

I'm going to give you topics. You'll set your timer for two minutes. Once the timer starts, you'll write a list of as many items that fall under that topic that you can. The more you let yourself go and just write down everything that comes to mind, the more this exercise will help. There are absolutely no wrong answers. Zero. Whatever you write down is correct, I promise. This is a great time to try and let your inner writer take the wheel and start to run wild. Maybe when I ask you to write down characters, like I will in a moment, your inner writer gives the answer PINEAPPLE. Well, I guess you're going to write that down! Seriously! Don't worry about making sense, you can work all of that out later.

I recommend writing these lists in a notebook so you can find them again later. In future exercises in this book, they'll come in handy anytime you need to figure out a dramatic element like character or setting before you begin. Turn to these lists if you ever find yourself stuck. When I was in grad school at San Francisco State University, my professor Peter Sinn Nachtrieb had me and my peers do something very much like this on our first day of class. I still go back to the lists I wrote that day, searching to see if anything I brainstormed in that first class, my very own garden of ideas, has ripened. Perhaps it's ready for the picking.

Writing Cue ❯❯

- Get your writing tools.
- Unlike what you wrote down for the brain drain, you'll want to keep these lists someplace easy to find later for inspiration.
- Set a two-minute timer for each list.
- Remember:
    - There are no wrong answers!
    - Don't think, just write!

1. Characters

Include enough detail to have a picture of who this character might be. You might want to include name, age, gender, occupation, or current predicament. Press GO on your two-minute timer and write as many characteristics as you can.

Examples:

- Mona, an eight-year-old girl looking for a lost dog
- Man in hotdog costume
- Evil Easter Bunny

2. Physical Actions

Get your timer ready. Two minutes on the clock! This time you'll be writing down physical actions any character might take. Ready, set, GO!

Examples:

- Slap
- Cartwheel
- Fold laundry

3. Items You Can Hold in Your Hand

Get your timer ready. Two minutes on the clock! Start thinking up items that folks can hold in their hands. Feel free to just write down as many of the objects in the room with you as you can. GO!

Examples:

- Sports trophy
- Stapler
- Hamster wheel

4. Items You Would Be Hard-Pressed to Hold in Your Hand

Get your timer ready. Two minutes on the clock! This time think of objects/things that you'd be hard-pressed to pick up. GO!

Examples:

- Yellow school bus

- Refrigerator
- Boulder

5. Places

Get your timer ready. Two minutes on the clock! What are some specific settings and places you can think of? Write down as many as you can! GO!

Examples:

- Laundromat
- Sea of Tranquility
- Playground with only one functioning swing
- San Diego, California

6. Time

Get your timer ready. Two minutes on the clock! *When* things take place has a lot of impact on *how* they unfold. Say you're writing a scene where one person asks another to help them bake a cake. That scene will change considerably if you set it at 5 a.m. compared to 5 p.m., or midnight compared to noon. Ready? GO!

Examples:

- High noon
- Swim practice
- Last five minutes of school before summer break
- 2:15 a.m.

7. One- or Two-Syllable Words

Get your timer ready. Two minutes on the clock! What are some short words you just love to use and say? Don't think too much about it, don't be logical. Words with one or two syllables that evoke some kind of feeling in you. GO!

Examples:

- Puppy
- Soup
- Flick

8. Luxury Words

Get your timer ready. Two minutes on the clock! What words feel luxurious coming off your tongue? These are not words you use every day, but when you do throw them into conversations, you feel fancy. **Reminder: don't worry about spelling in this or any brainstorm!** That's what spell-check is for later. The important part is to let your mind get out as many luxury words as possible! GO!

Examples:

- Penultimate
- Flabbergasted
- Assuage
- Ennui

9. Topics of Interest

Get your timer ready. Two minutes on the clock! What are you interested in? What gets you to wake up and lean in? These topics can and should range. GO!

Examples:

- Salem Witch Trials
- Bubonic plague
- Pacific Ocean

10. Questions

Finally! We're at the last brainstorming topic! Well done! Get your timer ready. Two minutes on the clock! I want you to list as many questions you can think of. These can include questions that have answers and questions that can't be answered. GO!

Examples:

- Cats or dogs?
- What came first, the chicken or the egg?
- What's around the next corner?

Interval

- Stand, stretch, move, shake it out.
- Look over your lists:
    - Star or underline your favorite answers in each category.

    - If you're in a group or class, have folks share their favorite answers.
- Keep these lists handy, they will help if you get stuck with future exercises!

Repeat as often as is helpful. Writing lists with a timer is a great way to get around your brain and unleash the writer that lives inside you. If you run through the above topics and need more, just know that the sky's the limit! You can write lists of your own creation. Anything that you think will help your inner writer. How many pizza toppings can you name in two minutes? Dog breeds? Types of cheese? What if you wrote a list of possible other LISTS you could make?

SPOTLIGHT ON UNLEASH

Unleashing the writer will make writing plays less like pulling teeth and more like being set loose at the dog park. Freedom! Excitement! Giving yourself regular **brain drain** and **brainstorming** time will strengthen that inner writer so they're ready to run when you're ready to write, but these exercises can also help before, during, or after any writing sessions!

Whenever I'm at a place where concentration eludes me, I take five minutes and do a brain drain. It's amazing how freeing it is once whatever has been bopping around my head is out on the page. And I turn to brainstorming whenever I'm stuck. I write lists of potential names when I don't know what to call a character, I list potential events when I'm not sure what will happen next, and with nearly all of my plays, I list potential titles until one falls out of my brain that I love. The greatest gift of writing is that there's always rewriting when we make a choice that doesn't work.

Try these tools out, then go out and find a few of your own. Remember, it takes practice to let yourself go. Once you find your favorite unleashing tools, figure out a schedule and practice regularly and often. Most importantly, remember that these exercises are not for thinking! Let the words fall out on the page. Repeat after me: don't think, just write!

OBJECTIVE

NOW THAT WE'VE DIPPED OUR TOES IN, it's time to dive into the elements of dramatic writing. The first, and I would argue the most essential, is **objective**.

Theatre first pulled me in as a performer. In college I was taught to approach each role with questions, the first always being: what does my character want? I haven't acted in years, but I still bring that first lesson to my writing.

My acting professor Juan Castro, who we called "Coach," told our class that we always want something. All of us, all the time. At first I didn't believe him. It felt callous. Selfish. I was a good person, I certainly didn't have ulterior motives behind all of my interactions! But as I started to pay more attention, I realized wanting was all around.

Let's turn to the purest want-machines around: babies. They cry because they want something. They want food, or a clean diaper, or entertainment, or to see your face, or less clothing, or a blanket, or just to see your reaction, or, or, or. Babies are little beings of nonstop want. They don't have language yet and so they cry, forcing their scene partners (aka their caregivers) to try and provide whatever their objective happens to be this time. When the baby cries, caregivers often start with changing the diaper. Baby still crying? I guess that wasn't their objective. Let's try something to eat next. Still crying? Okay, maybe they have gas and need to be burped. No? The caregiver will move on to the other objective possibilities until the crying stops. And you'll notice that not only does the baby have an objective here, but so does the caregiver. They want the baby to stop crying, and having had two babies of my own,

I can say with authority this was my main objective for most of their baby years.

This brings us back to my professor's statement, "*Every*one wants something *all* the time." Both sides of any interaction have an objective. After all, in that very class, my professor wanted to teach me, and I wanted to learn. Whether we realize it or not, we want something, and so does everyone else. To me, since it's both sides of any interaction, it becomes universal, and the thought of selfishness or callousness just disappears. It's not terrible to always want something, it's just a fact of being.

So . . . We all want things. Objectives, we got 'em, whether we're aware of them or not. So if we want our characters to reflect human nature on the page, they need to want something too. The pursuit of the objective not only makes them compelling to watch, but more importantly, gives them dramatic action, which we will talk about later. Hamlet wants to know if his uncle murdered his father. Oedipus wants to save his people from the plague. Lysistrata wants to stop the war. Juliet wants to be with Romeo. These characters are driven by their objectives in every single interaction throughout each of their respective plays.

FIND THE OBJECTIVE

What's your favorite book? Favorite movie? Play? TV show? One of the writing superpowers you may not even realize you have is that you have already seen a LOT of examples of the concepts and tools we're going to be covering. I want you to think back to the stories that have really grabbed you, the ones you think about for days or weeks after. We don't have to only look to real life to understand objectives, because the stories you love are rich with examples. So think of your favorite stories, and the characters in those stories. Get a few examples in your head, then try and identify what those characters want.

- Start a list!
  - How many characters and their **objectives** can you think of?
  - Examples include:
    - Macbeth wants to be king
    - Medea wants revenge on her husband, Jason
    - Cookie Monster wants cookies
- Let your examples vary as much as your brain will allow! There are no examples too silly.
- If you're in a group or class, have volunteers share examples.

Next time you crack open a book, or are in front of a screen watching something, try to figure out what those characters want right in the moment. It's a great practice that can pay off later when you start wrestling with your characters and all the way they go after their objectives.

TANGIBLE OBJECTIVE MONOLOGUE

To show you an example of a character that wants, I have a monologue for you. There will be quite a few example monologues and scenes throughout this book, all set in the backstage world of a *Romeo and Juliet* production. I wrote these scenes and monologues specifically for this book. My aim is to zero in on each specific tool, show how it works, and give you the space to play with it. My reasoning? Well, let's say you walked into a kitchen with zero culinary experience and tried to make pizza for the first time, having only eaten pizza once. That would be pretty challenging—even just the pizza dough alone! That's why we have recipes. Guides that take a large and complicated process and break it down into pieces you can tackle one at a time. If there was a recipe for writing a play, objectives would be a main ingredient, as would be the other tools that will follow. Think of these example monologues and scenes as practice in using these ingredients, like tasting your dish along the way as you cook. The point is to concentrate on the pieces, to better understand how they work together in the whole.

Now let's jump into that example of objective! We'll start with an objective that the character can pick up and hold, i.e. a tangible objective.

- Read the monologue out loud.
- Try to identify what the character wants as you read.

(STAGE MANAGER moves to a table set up with various breakfast treats, surveys the scene, and then approaches an individual who's just picked up a treat.)

STAGE MANAGER: You don't know me yet. I'm the Stage Manager. For the play. The play we're putting on. You know, *Romeo and Juliet*? Hahahaha, obviously you know or you wouldn't be here. I really should have gotten name tags. Anyway, this is a little awkward, but you're holding my breakfast. I know you didn't do it on purpose, and I'm not mad or anything. Really. You had no idea that muffin was my muffin, how could you? It's on a table with at least a dozen others, and it's not like it had a sign with "reserved for Stage Manager" on it. But it's mine. And I want it. You might think it's unfair, but what you have to understand is that I have been awake since 5 a.m. this morning. Someone had to print the scripts. Someone had to print the contracts. Someone had to print and hang up the new policies on lateness and inappropriate behavior. Someone had to go to Costco and buy snacks and breakfast treats for this first rehearsal. And sure, that someone could have been given a lot more notice than a frantic phone call at 5 this morning, but you know what? They didn't. So that someone, ME, got up and got to work. And I haven't stopped working since. A little more warning would have been nice, but I got it done. Why? Because the show must go on and the show can't go on if it never started the first rehearsal, that's why. And I can handle it. Of course I can. I'm a Stage Manager, after all, I was made to handle it. But, I have needs. And, back to the point of this conversation: you are holding the very last lemon poppy seed muffin in your hand right now. The last of twelve, I know because I set them out this morning after buying them first thing from Costco when they opened. I haven't had time to eat until right now, this very moment. I have five minutes before rehearsal starts and if I don't eat now I won't have another chance until 2:30, and trust me when I tell you that that would not be good for our first day together. I need that muffin. I want it. Feel free to have one of the blueberry muffins, or go crazy with a chocolate chocolate chip muffin. But that muffin, the one in your hand, that's mine. It is MY MUFFIN! *(Grabs the muffin.)* Thank you. This is going to be such a FUN show, don't you think? . . . *(To everyone in the room:)* Five minutes, everyone! Five minutes!

(They take a big bite of the muffin.)

› Scene Study ‹

- What tangible things does the Stage Manager want?
    - Either write your answer down, or open the question up for a group discussion.

I start with the tangible because it can be helpful to have a clear physical object that a character wants. Something they can pick up and see: Beth wants a chocolate cupcake, Owen wants a new red t-shirt, Sally wants the twenty-foot-tall skeleton from Home Depot (me too, Sally, me too). Tangible objectives are clear-cut: not only can we imagine our characters with these things, it is clear if they are successful obtaining them or not. In the example above, the Stage Manager gets the lemon poppy seed muffin, and so they have achieved their objective. You can't always separate tangible and intangible objectives, as they often get mixed up together, but I wouldn't worry about trying. Look at the example above: not only does the Stage Manager want that lemon poppy seed muffin, they also want the person they're taking it from to know that they deserve it, that they earned that muffin.

Writing Cue ➤➤

Write a monologue where one character wants a tangible object from another. Every word out of their mouth should be aimed to achieve their goal. I'd recommend setting a timer between five and ten minutes. Don't let your hands stop writing until the timer goes off. You can use the lemon poppy seed muffin as your objective, as well as the Stage Manager character above; or you can go back to your **brainstorming** lists from the first chapter and pick from there; or you can make both things up right now! To summarize, you will need:

- Two characters: one character who speaks, and a second, silent character being spoken to.
- An object that is your speaking character's **objective**.

Don't worry about coming up with the very best idea: just go with the first thing that pops in your head. It won't be perfect; it doesn't even have to be good. Good isn't our objective. Our objective is to learn more about characters wanting things.

Get your writing tools and a timer ready! Put a time between five and ten minutes on the clock and GO!

Here are some deeper questions to keep you going if you get stuck:

- What is the object? How does the character who wants it describe it?
- Why does your character want this object?
- What does it mean for your character not to have this object?

❮ Interval ❯

- Stop writing once the timer goes off.
- Stand, stretch, move, shake it out.
- How did that feel?
    - Did anything surprise you while you were writing?
    - Was anything easier than you expected it to be?
    - Was anything trickier than you expected it to be?
- Read your monologue out loud. I promise, it's not weird at all. The goal for what we write is, after all, to have actors eventually recite it in front of an audience. The words were written *to* be spoken. So much can be learned from this very private reading. Reading your work out loud allows you to preview how your words sound. You may find jokes you didn't know were there, word combinations that trip up the tongue in unintentional ways, or many other insights. I read all my work out loud to myself in my office with only my two sleeping dogs as audience, so

you'll be in good company! Or, if you're in a group, have volunteers share.

- ◦ What did your character want?

INTANGIBLE OBJECTIVE MONOLOGUE

After tackling tangible objects with our Stage Manager and their lemon poppy seed muffin, we're going to look at a new character and an example of an **intangible objective**. An **intangible objective** isn't something you can physically hold or see. We constantly want intangible things from other people: respect, forgiveness, freedom, acceptance. A lot of our objectives are intangible; it would be simpler if our objectives were limited to just a million dollars, a chocolate cupcake, or that twenty-foot-tall skeleton, but the world isn't that simple, and our characters shouldn't be either.

- Read the monologue out loud.
- Try to identify what the character wants as you read.

(DIRECTOR grabs ASSISTANT STAGE MANAGER and pulls them aside.)

DIRECTOR: Hey. You're the Assistant Stage Manager, right? Good to meet you. I'm the Director. And I need . . . well . . . assistance. Look, we haven't even started the first rehearsal and there have been whispers, all about *me* and my choices for the play. Can you believe that? The nerve, right? It shouldn't matter that this is my first time directing, the director *should* have respect! I'm the leader, aren't I? *I* was the one who wrote the proposal to direct this play, *I* was the one with the vision, the *moxie*, to suggest that as a first-time director I could handle one of the most famous plays of all time. I'm not saying it's not intimidating, I know that every audience member will be comparing this production to their favorite *Romeo and Juliet* film adaptation, I get that, and I feel the pressure, I'm not trying to pretend that I don't. But, and I don't say this lightly, I believe a mutiny is afoot. And I know in my bones that this production will not survive if the creative team doesn't fall into line with my vision. A house divided cannot stand. And that's where you come in. Pledge me your loyalty and lend me your eyes and ears. You will be my spy. After rehearsal each day you will report back every word against me that you hear and every eye rolled behind my back. And I need you to keep extra eyes on the Stage Manager. I know, I get it, that could get awkward for you, but just remember it's for the greater good of keeping *me* in charge! And you will be rewarded for your loyalty, trust in that. As a matter of fact, why don't you go and grab an extra muffin from the table before we start rehearsal. The snacks were all my idea, by the way, not that anyone has said "thank you." But we'll have the last laugh, won't we, comrade? Oh yes. Yes we will.

Scene Study

- What does the Director want?
    - What are they trying to get from the Assistant Stage Manager?
- Go back through the monologue, underline everything the Director says that identifies what they want.

Writing Cue >>

For this exercise, you'll write a monologue where one character wants something intangible from another. Something you cannot touch or feel or pick up, as in a piece of information, or approval, or sympathy. Since we haven't yet brainstormed a list of potential intangible objectives, let's take two minutes now so we don't feel stuck when it's monologue-writing time.

Examples:

- Comfort
- Superiority
- Knowledge

Get your timer ready. Two minutes on the clock! I want you to write down as many **intangible objectives** as you can think of. Ready? GO!

Finished with your list? Fantastic. Take a second and look through all the intangible objectives you just wrote down and pick one that jumps out to you, or use "loyalty" from the Director's monologue up above. I want you to have two characters again, and one will deliver a monologue in order to achieve their objective. To summarize, this monologue will include:

- An **intangible objective**.
- Two character: one character who speaks, and a second, silent character being spoken to.

Get your writing tools and timer ready. Put a time between five and ten minutes on the clock! GO!

If you get stuck, here are some questions you can answer in your monologue:

- What does the character want?
- Why does your character want this?
- Why do they want it from the character they're talking to?
- What does it mean for your character if they fail?
- What does it mean to your character if they succeed?

❮ Interval ❯

- Stop writing once the timer goes off.
- Stand, stretch, move, shake it out.
- How did that feel?
    - Did anything surprise you while you were writing?
    - Was anything easier than you expected it to be?
    - Was anything trickier than you expected it to be?
- Read your monologue out loud, or if you're in a group, have volunteers share.
    - What did your character want?

MICRO- VS. MACRO-OBJECTIVES

I just had you write two monologues; each of those monologues contained a **micro-objective**. When we think of anything micro, we're thinking small, specific. It's helpful to think small, specifically when you're first playing with objectives. Just like it's helpful to walk before you run. When I first realized that I wanted to write plays, I challenged myself to write a short play a day for an entire month. I'd make up a character and a small, specific objective, and then write, trying my hardest not to think, and just let words fall out onto the page like I'm asking you to do with these exercises. Eventually we're going to move on from these exercises and start to put together an entire play. Within a play, a character will have two different types of "objectives"; they'll have many, many micro-objectives that they pursue throughout each scene of the play, and one single, big, main **MACRO-objective**.

A **macro-objective** is the giant, ultimate goal: to win over the love of your life, to successfully rob the bank, to become a professional concert pianist. These giant goals contain many smaller micro-objectives along the way.

We'll tackle macro-objectives in much greater detail in Act Two, when we dive into structure. Plays are like a knitted scarf: when you pull on one thread, you'll often get a whole lot more than you bargained for. Objectives, and more specifically, macro-objectives, are tied heavily to how you structure a play, which is tied heavily to character, which is tied heavily to the small, specific micro-objectives found in each scene within that play.

For now, focus on the small, the specific. After you've had time to play and build up your understanding of the tiny pieces, we'll zoom out and explore the big picture.

SPOTLIGHT ON OBJECTIVE

Objectives are the foundation of dramatic writing. Everything builds out from there. Objectives tell us about the character, shape a story, and allow our audience to invest. Moving forward, you'll see that every other tool or element I break down relates to objectives. When I read or see a play, whether it's a first draft, in a classroom, or on a professional stage, the first question I always ask myself is: **what did the characters want?** When I set out on a new project, I think about what objective will put a character in the position to tell the story I want to tell.

In my full-length, myth-inspired fantasy *Of Serpents and Sea Spray,* the main character Iro, a young orphan, wants to locate the one and only flying horse, Pegasus. The performers from the circus she's accidentally joined want free labor. And Iro's poor, worried Uncle wants nothing more than a safe and sound niece. These objectives drive this story, each turn and every twist. And that makes sense—after all, objectives drive everything that happens offstage as well.

ACTION

EVERYTHING CHARACTERS DO in order to achieve their **objective** is **action**. They're two sides of the same coin. If it wasn't for a character actively working to achieve their objective, how would the audience know that they have an objective? It is with the character's action, their working toward their goal, that we as an audience can fully see their objective. Characters take action in order to get what they want, and the reverse is also true: a character without an objective doesn't have much to do onstage.

WHAT IS ACTION?

Action is what a character does. Think about the verbs a character would use as they move toward an objective. Say Juliet has an objective to complete a jigsaw puzzle. What actions could Juliet take to accomplish this? She might take physical actions, like FLIPPING pieces around to see how they fit together or SEARCHING for a particular piece. She might also take non-physical actions, like STUDYING the box or ASKING other people for help.

Action is shown in both **dialogue** and **stage directions**. Using the jigsaw-puzzle example, I could write stage directions like:

> *(JULIET **opens** the jigsaw-puzzle box, then **dumps** the contents onto a table. JULIET **flips** all of the pieces that landed face down. JULIET **searches** for corner pieces, **moving** them when she finds one to where she imagines they'll fit.)*

All of these action words, or verbs, are moving Juliet closer to reaching her objective, a completed puzzle. Stage directions are an essential tool for showing the actions of your characters, but since we're working toward writing plays, the bulk of our characters' **physical actions** will often be stage directions, while their **non-physical actions** will often be dialogue. Every art form tells stories in a way that's specific to the medium. Movies and TV shows share stories through pictures, while plays share stories through dialogue. Movies and TV can change locations in a snap, they can zoom up close or zoom out far away from their subjects. We *watch* movies and TV. Visuals are what movies and TV have in high demand. But we *listen* to plays. Dialogue delivers vital information to the audience: where we are, who we are, what we want, and how we are trying to get what we want. So, how can Juliet actively work toward her objective through verbal speech? The options are infinite, but here are a few examples of what Juliet might say:

JULIET: O Romeo, Romeo, let's bond over completing this beautiful puzzle together!

Or:

JULIET: Help me! Someone help me! I HAVE TO FINISH THIS JIGSAW PUZZLE BEFORE 3 P.M. OR THE THEATER WILL EXPLODE!

In both examples of dialogue, Juliet is actively working toward her objective, though her method varies wildly. She's not moving her body, but she's still active. Active characters captivate our attention onstage, often needing to employ both physical and non-physical actions in order to get what they want. I think it's time we think up a few examples . . .

FIND THE ACTION

Think of that favorite book, TV show, movie, or play. How do their characters go after their objectives? What actions do they take?

- Pick a book, movie, TV show, or play that you know very well.
- Pick one character, and starting from the beginning, list all of the different **actions** they use in order to reach their **objective**.
    - When are their actions **physical**? Like stage directions?
    - When are their actions not **physical**? Like dialogue?
- Repeat with as many of the different characters as you'd like.

PHYSICAL AND NON-PHYSICAL ACTION SCENE

In art, and in life, action can be physical and non-physical. Here's a scene demonstrating two characters who both have objectives and are actively working to achieve their objectives. One uses physical means, the other non-physical.

- Read the scene out loud:

(The costume shop. COSTUME DESIGNER and JULIET are onstage. COSTUME DESIGNER holds a soft measuring tape.)

COSTUME DESIGNER: Thanks for coming in, this shouldn't take long. I just need to take your measurements.

JULIET: Yeah, cool. Sounds good.

COSTUME DESIGNER: Okay. Raise your arms.

JULIET: Yeah.

(JULIET does not raise her arms.)

COSTUME DESIGNER: Um . . . You don't have to be nervous or anything. I'm not going to bite.

JULIET: No, of course not.

COSTUME DESIGNER: Great. Arms up then.

JULIET: I wasn't supposed to get the part.

COSTUME DESIGNER: I'm sorry?

JULIET: Juliet. I wasn't. I wasn't supposed to get the part of Juliet.

COSTUME DESIGNER: Oh.

JULIET: Yeah. OH. I'm just . . . You know what? I'm just going to go.

(COSTUME DESIGNER blocks the exit.)

COSTUME DESIGNER: You can't leave. I just, I'm just going to take your measurements.

JULIET: But that's not all! You're going to take my measurements and then you're going to make me a *costume,* which I will have to wear in front of *people*. LOTS of PEOPLE.

COSTUME DESIGNER: Well, yeah. Hopefully.

JULIET: I am not hopeful! Not for that!

COSTUME DESIGNER: You should be! We want people to see the play!

JULIET: Not me! I want no one to see this play.

COSTUME DESIGNER: Look, you're nervous. I get that. That's normal.

JULIET: It is?

COSTUME DESIGNER: Sure. Probably. Anyway, bring your nerves to the Director. Not to me. The Director deals with nerves, I just handle costumes.

JULIET: I wasn't supposed to get the part.

COSTUME DESIGNER: That's what you said.

JULIET: I only auditioned to get my mom off my back. "You never try new things!" She's always saying, "You don't have any friends!" I wanted to get cast as a tree or something.

COSTUME DESIGNER: I don't think there is a tree in *Romeo and Juliet.*

JULIET: Well there should be! I would kill that part!

COSTUME DESIGNER: You know, I think you'd feel better about all of this if you just raise your arms up.

JULIET: Don't you try to trick me.

COSTUME DESIGNER: I'm not. I'm just, you know, on a time crunch. This is theatre.

JULIET: I should have just volunteered to be on one of the crews. Like costumes! I could be helping you with the costumes!

COSTUME DESIGNER: Yeah, again, topic of conversation for the Director. Arms. Up. Now.

JULIET: Well then, maybe I should just go and find—

COSTUME DESIGNER: You're not leaving this room before I get your measurements.

JULIET: You aren't terribly kind. Did you know that?

COSTUME DESIGNER: Yeah, well I wanted to play Juliet. Arms. Up. NOW.

(JULIET raises her hands. End of scene.)

➤ Scene Study ❮

- Going through the scene, note down every **action** taken by the Costume Designer.
- Go back again, and this time focus on Juliet, noting down her **action** shifts.
    - Are there different ways these **actions** could be described?
- If you're in a group, have volunteers share their findings.
    - Does anyone describe these **actions** differently?

Writing Cue ➤➤

For this exercise, you'll write a two-person scene. Both characters have **objectives**. At least one of the characters uses **physical actions** in order to obtain their objective, and at least one character will use **non-physical actions**. Before we get going though, let's brainstorm some non-physical actions. We already have a list of physical actions from earlier. Have both lists handy in case you find yourself stuck, or your characters become inactive.

Two minutes on the clock! I want you to write down as many **non-physical actions** as you can think of. Ready? GO!

Examples:

- Intimidate
- Plead
- Beguile

All set with your list? Great! As you move to the scene, a reminder that this scene will include:

- Two characters. You can make these up, grab them from your earlier lists, or use the characters above.
- Both characters will have **objectives**.
- Have one or both characters use a **physical action**.
- Have one or both characters use a **non-physical action**.

Get your timer ready! Put a time between five and ten minutes on the clock! GO!

❮ Interval ❯

- Once the timer sounds, stop writing!
- Stand, stretch, move, shake it out.
- How did that feel?
    - Was anything surprising?
    - Was anything harder than you expected? Easier than expected?
- Read your own scene out loud, playing both characters. If you're in a group, have volunteers share their scenes.
    - Identify the **actions** used by the characters.

SHOWING CHARACTER THROUGH ACTION: SCENE ONE

Action not only shows our audience that our characters have objectives, but it also shows the characters' personalities, their relationship to other characters, and how important their objectives are. To see this in action, let's take a two-character scene written two ways. Both characters will have the same objective for both iterations, but we'll change the actions of one of the characters to see how that affects their personality and their relationship with the other character.

(The greenroom. PARIS paces. HEAD OF PUBLICITY enters.)

HEAD OF PUBLICITY: I just talked to the Director.

PARIS: And?

HEAD OF PUBLICITY: And the cast will stay as is. No role switching.

PARIS: Unbelievable. UNbeLIEVABLE! I can't believe it. Can you believe it?

HEAD OF PUBLICITY: It's beyond comprehension.

PARIS: It really is. And here I was thinking that the Director's main job was to put on the best show possible. I don't really see that happening with someone else as Romeo.

HEAD OF PUBLICITY: Absolutely! It's like they want this whole production to fail before the first week of rehearsals is through.

PARIS: I should be Romeo.

HEAD OF PUBLICITY: I know!

PARIS: Paris is a terrible part. Paris is like, he's almost the villain! I'm not a villain!

HEAD OF PUBLICITY: You are SO not a villain.

PARIS: Something must be done.

HEAD OF PUBLICITY: I've already been thinking about how we should handle this. I think it's time we take advantage of my position here. I'm the head of publicity, right?

PARIS: Yeah, and?

HEAD OF PUBLICITY: Well, maybe there's a skeleton or two in Romeo's closet that I can make public!

PARIS: That's diabolical! I love it!

HEAD OF PUBLICITY: Right? Why not use all the ammo at our disposal? With so much on the line? You were born for the role of Romeo!

PARIS: OR . . .

HEAD OF PUBLICITY: Or?

PARIS: Or we blackmail Romeo to give the part up!

HEAD OF PUBLICITY: That's even better!

PARIS: That way we don't sully the production or theater.

HEAD OF PUBLICITY: Genius!

PARIS: And if that doesn't work . . .

HEAD OF PUBLICITY: Yeah?

PARIS: We'll make his life here as painful as possible.

HEAD OF PUBLICITY: Oh? How would we do that?

PARIS: The usual ways. Move his props, turn the cast against him, maybe let the air out of his tires. You still have your cat, right?

HEAD OF PUBLICITY: Fluffball is alive and well!

PARIS: Good. We'll need some cat hair. I have it on good authority that he's incredibly allergic to cats!

HEAD OF PUBLICITY: Fluffball is getting groomed next week! I'll ask the groomer to bag up all the extra hair!

PARIS: I knew I could count on you . . . Now, I have to run to rehearsal. You start digging!

HEAD OF PUBLICITY: Aye aye, Captain!

(End of scene.)

In the scene above we have the actor playing Paris and the Head of Publicity for *Romeo and Juliet.* What changes if we tweak one of their actions?

SHOWING CHARACTER THROUGH ACTION: SCENE TWO

- Read the scene out loud:

(The greenroom. PARIS paces. HEAD OF PUBLICITY enters.)

HEAD OF PUBLICITY: I just talked to the Director.

PARIS: And?

HEAD OF PUBLICITY: And the cast will stay as is. No role switching.

PARIS: Unbelievable. UNbeLIEVABLE! I can't believe it. Can you believe it?

HEAD OF PUBLICITY: I mean . . .

PARIS: What??

HEAD OF PUBLICITY: It's just, you've had a lot of big parts. Back-to-back-to-back, maybe it's time for someone else—

PARIS: But Paris is basically the villain? Are you saying I'm the villain?

HEAD OF PUBLICITY: No, but you weren't upset when you were cast as Iago.

PARIS: That's different, that was SO different!

HEAD OF PUBLICITY: Because Paris is a smaller part?

PARIS: What? No. Obviously no!

HEAD OF PUBLICITY: Because Iago is most definitely the villain in *Othello.*

PARIS: Yes, obviously. But it's a totally different play! And anyway, I was born to play Romeo! Before auditions you thought I was a shoo-in!

HEAD OF PUBLICITY: I did think you had a very good chance . . .

PARIS: See? This has to be some terrible mistake!

HEAD OF PUBLICITY: But I *just* talked to the Director for you, and I was *just* assured that not only was this not a mistake, but that no changes would be made.

PARIS: That can't be it. There has to be a way! Something we can do!

HEAD OF PUBLICITY: I think the only thing to do at this point is to start memorizing your Paris lines.

PARIS: OR! Or, you could dig dirt up on Romeo? We could force him into giving the part up! I mean, especially if it comes from you, that would be a serious threat. With your gift for social media, we could really get the word out!

HEAD OF PUBLICITY: Blackmail? Seriously?

PARIS: Don't exaggerate! Not blackmail at all. We'll just be using something against someone so they do what we want.

HEAD OF PUBLICITY: That's blackmail.

PARIS: Okay, then I guess yes! Blackmail. Are you in?

HEAD OF PUBLICITY: No.

PARIS: Okay, if blackmail doesn't work for you, what if we pick on Romeo until he leaves the production?

HEAD OF PUBLICITY: That might be worse?

PARIS: It'll be mostly light-hearted pranks. You know, hiding props, maybe letting the air out of his tires. Funny stuff!

HEAD OF PUBLICITY: No!

PARIS: What if you gather up hair from your cat and we leave it all over his costume? I've heard he's super allergic!

HEAD OF PUBLICITY: Don't bring Fluffball into this!

PARIS: Okay, then how about—

HEAD OF PUBLICITY: Stop. Please. Look, I wanted you to get the part too. I thought you were the best choice. But I'm not the Director. I think you'll be better off letting this all go and doing your best as Paris.

PARIS: But what if we—

HEAD OF PUBLICITY: NO!

(HEAD OF PUBLICITY exits.)

PARIS: But you didn't let me explain! You'll like this one I think, really!

(End of scene.)

Scene Study

- How does changing the Head of Publicity's **action** change their character?
- How does changing the **action** change their relationship to Paris?
- What are the differences between the two scenes?

Writing Cue >>

Now it's your turn to experiment with showing character through action! To begin, identify your two characters and their objectives. Feel free to look back to your lists from the first chapter, or completely steal and rewrite the scene from above. For this first scene, you will need:

- Two characters.
- **Objectives** for both characters.
- **Actions** these characters take in order to get what they want. These can be **physical** or **non-physical**.

Set a timer for at least five minutes. Timer ready? Great! Time to write! GO!

- Once your timer goes off, stop!
- Stand, stretch, move, shake it out.
- How did that feel?
- Ready to completely turn the scene on its head?

Now rewrite your scene! Select one of your characters and change their action, while leaving their objective the same. This will affect your other character, so don't worry if they change as well. For this new iteration, you will need:

- The same two characters.
- The same **objectives** for both characters.
- New **actions** for at least ONE of your characters.

Get your timer ready for at least five minutes, and don't stop until your timer sounds. Timer ready? Time to write! GO!

❮ Interval ❯

- Once the timer sounds, stop writing!
- Stand, stretch, move, shake it out.
- How did that feel?
    - Was anything surprising?
    - Was anything harder than you expected? Easier than expected?
- Read your own scene out loud, playing both characters, or if you're in a group, have volunteers share.
    - What do the **actions** the characters use tell you about who they are?
    - What do the **actions** tell you about their relationship?

ENCORE: OUR OWN WORST ENEMY

Welcome to your first "**encore**" topic! These encore sections are for anyone who wants to dig deeper and give themselves a challenge.

In real life, our actions sometimes hamper our attempts to reach our objectives, instead of help. Maybe we're cast in a play and our objective is to do our best in the role. All of that is well and good until you want to see a movie with friends instead of learning lines. We're great at working against our own interests. And this should be reflected in the characters we put onstage. Some will also be better at working against themselves than others.

ENCORE: COUNTERINTUITIVE ACTION SCENE

Let's return to those folks putting on a production of *Romeo and Juliet* to see an example of characters working against themselves. As you listen or read, identify objectives, actions, and when the character's action isn't helping them get closer to their objective.

(Outside the theater, JULIET enters from a theater exit. She pulls out keys. NURSE enters from the same theater exit.)

NURSE: Rehearsal is about to start! Where are you going?

JULIET: Oh, I, uh, I left, um, stuff, something I really need, it's in my car.

NURSE: Can't you get it later? The Director will flip if you're not there!

JULIET: Oh, but I'll be back. I'm just going to my car for, uh, that thing.

NURSE: I heard that you have a bit of stage fright?

JULIET: What? Who would say that? That's, that's flat-out bonkers! And wrong. So wrong.

NURSE: It's okay, you know. It's not a big deal.

JULIET: You don't think so?

NURSE: No, lots of people get stage fright.

JULIET: You think?

NURSE: Oh yeah, tons. Pretty sure it's up there with the most common fears.

JULIET: I didn't want as big a role as *Juliet*, you know? I didn't expect— I thought I'd play a nonspeaking part! Like a tree!

NURSE: Relax, we'll get you through this.

JULIET: You will?

NURSE: For sure. The show must go on! And I'm the expert on combating stage fright!

JULIET: Then you've dealt with it too?

NURSE: Me? No. Never. Not my style.

JULIET: Oh.

NURSE: But I do know a lot of things you should be MORE scared of than just talking in front of strangers.

JULIET: Oh, well I don't think—

NURSE: Like, for example, did you know that a surprising number of people DIE onstage?

JULIET: What?

NURSE: Just boom. Dead! Mostly choking. It's surprisingly hard to eat and drink onstage. But you don't have to eat or drink ANYthing, so you won't have to worry about that!

JULIET: . . . Okay . . .

NURSE: And you're probably concerned about learning all those lines, *Juliet* has A LOT of lines!

JULIET: Yeah, that's another concerning—

NURSE: Don't worry about lines. They aren't a big deal.

JULIET: I'm pretty sure they've a *very* big deal.

NURSE: Well, I almost never remember my lines and I've been in tons of shows before!

JULIET: Really?

NURSE: You bet! And with a play like this? Do you know how popular *Romeo and Juliet* is? The audience will already know what happens! So if we mess up, they'll just fill in the gaps.

JULIET: They will?

NURSE: Totally! And, most of the other actors are great at memorization. If you get stuck, they'll help you get through it with ad-libbing and stuff.

JULIET: Don't . . . Um . . . Don't you and I have a pretty big scene together?

NURSE: Do we? Huh. To be honest, I have not read the script yet.

JULIET: Oh. Right. Well then . . .

(JULIET inches to exit to the parking lot. NURSE stops her, then puts an arm around her.)

NURSE: I'm glad we had the time for this chat! I'm sure you feel much much better about all of this now!

JULIET: Oh, well, actually, I still need that something out of my car, and it might take me a while to find it, so I better run—

NURSE: You'll get whatever it is after rehearsal. Oh! And speaking of your car, can I get a ride home after rehearsal? And then a ride to rehearsal tomorrow? And then a ride home after? I actually hate the bus, so can I get a ride for the rest of the rehearsals and then shows?

JULIET: Um, uh . . .

(NURSE leads JULIET back toward the theater.)

NURSE: Great! Thanks! And I have lots more facts and tidbits to help you, if your stage fright ever pops up again. I know every death that happened on our stage! Did you know there's a soft spot on the stage floor? Yeah, you'll be feeling better about acting in no time!

(NURSE and JULIET exit back into the theater. End of scene.)

➤ Scene Study ❮

- What is Juliet's **objective** or **objectives**?
- What is the Nurse's **objective** or **objectives**?
- What **actions** are Juliet taking in order to achieve her **objective(s)?**
    - Are they helping her to reach her **objective(s)?**
    - Are they hindering her from reaching her **objective(s)?**
- What **actions** is the Nurse taking in order to achieve her **objective(s)?**
    - Are they helping her to reach her **objective(s)?**
    - Are they hindering her from reaching her **objective(s)?**

Writing Cue ➤➤

Now it's your turn to have one of your characters work against their goal. Turn back to your lists of characters and actions to get inspired, or steal and rewrite the scene from above! In this scene, you will need:

- Two characters.
- Both with **objectives.**
- Both take **actions** in order to reach those **objectives.**
- At least one of your character's **actions** does not help them reach their **objectives,** in fact they're working against their goal.

Get a timer ready! Give yourself at least five minutes on your timer. Ready? GO!

❮ Interval ❯

- Once the timer sounds, stop writing!
- Stand, stretch, move, shake it out.
- How did that feel?
  - Was anything surprising?
  - Was anything harder than you expected? Easier than expected?
- Read your scene out loud, or if you're in a group, have volunteers share.
  - What were the characters' **objectives**?
  - What **actions** helped them reach their **objectives**, and which were working against their **objectives**?
  - Did they realize they weren't helping themselves reach their own **objectives**?
  - What information do we gain about the characters through their choices?

SPOTLIGHT ON ACTION

Action is essential. Not only does it show the audience your characters' objectives, it also shows us who they are, and their relationships with other characters. A character's action can manifest physically or non-physically. And sometimes, there are characters who employ action that works against their objective.

If you're stuck on a tricky scene, experiment by trying out different actions. There is a huge difference between the actions of requesting and demanding, for example, but they could easily be used toward the same objective. What happens when you push one of your characters to a more explicit action? Or more subtle? How does that change the other characters? The scene? The journey of the play as a whole? Action has the power to change everything.

And not only can action change everything, focusing on action, especially in a first draft, can free up imagination. Instead of worrying about all the things you want to put in, you can focus on one verb at a time. *My character needs to confess or punish or trick.* While your brain goes to work on that, you'll be amazed by everything else that will start to happen around the characters naturally, especially if you've been putting in the work to unleash. As an added bonus, focusing on one verb per character can also help you to create differing characters. In my play *The Hardy Girls,* two teen detectives Fran and Juno attempt to clear the name of their wrongly accused friend. And while they share that objective, the actions they employ vary wildly, resulting in two distinct characters. Because not only do we learn about objectives through action, we also learn about characters and their relationships as well.

Find actions that can give you confidence to jump into your characters' lives, their stories. Everyone learns from active characters: the audience, the performers, even you, the creator.

In fact, if you'd like a bonus writing cue, why don't you take one of the exercises you've written so far and give the character(s) different actions and rewrite it! Have a timer ready, and once you've selected your new actions, get to rewriting!

STAKES

WHAT DOES YOUR CHARACTER HAVE to gain? What do they have to lose? **Objective** is what our characters want, **action** is what our characters do in order to get what they want, and **stakes** are what is on the line. If we think back to objectives, and how everyone everywhere has an objective, all the time, stakes are really what give our audiences a reason to care about our characters' successes and failures.

WHAT'S ON THE LINE?

Just like with objectives and action, we can find stakes all around us in the real world too. Remember the baby and the caregiver? A baby has something they want—an objective. They take the action of crying to get it. The caregiver's objective is to figure out their baby's objective so they will stop crying. They take multiple actions to comfort the baby, to see which will make them cease crying. What is at stake in this situation? For both baby and caregiver, it's often being able to go back to sleep. Which, as anyone sleep deprived will tell you, is a lot on the line.

And we can see stakes all over, not just with babies. Ever stay up late studying for a big test? Or drop everything to help out a friend? Or exhibit care when moving something breakable? Or agonize over the wording of a text message to your crush? All of those situations come with stakes of their own as well. After all, what happens if you fail that big test? Or ignore that friend in need? Or drop a prized heirloom? Or accidentally confess you're head-over-heels in love with someone you met yesterday? Just like with objectives and action, because we experience stakes in our lives, we crave to see characters grapple with stakes of their own onstage.

FIND THE STAKES!

Greek mythology is a fantastic place to look for big stakes. Oedipus wants to save his people from the plague. What is at stake if he is not successful? His people get sick and die. If Lysistrata and her fellow women aren't successful at stopping the war, the war will continue and Spartans and Athenians will continue to die. Start a list of characters from your favorite stories, using either the characters you've explored in previous exercises, or a new set that you haven't yet put under the microscope. What is at stake for them?

- Start a list:
  - Write down characters and what is at **stake** for them.
  - How many can you think up?
  - Challenge yourself! Get a timer involved or give yourself a number to aim for.

As you consume media, identify what's at stake while you're watching or reading. I know it sounds like I'm giving you homework when you would otherwise be relaxing in front of a good story, and that's because I am. Writers are sponges, and we need to soak up and learn every chance we get. And the more you can identify these tools in other work, the easier it will be for you to use them on your own.

PLAYING WITH STAKES: SCENES ONE AND TWO

Let's go back to *Romeo and Juliet* and see stakes in action. As you read, think about what is at stake for each of these characters.

(JULIET sits on a sofa in the greenroom. ROMEO enters and sits next to her.)

ROMEO: Hey.

JULIET: Hey.

ROMEO: I heard you might quit the show.

JULIET: Yeah. I was thinking about it.

ROMEO: I don't think you should do that.

JULIET: Yeah?

ROMEO: Look, we don't have to go into a big thing or anything. Just, like, don't quit.

JULIET: How come? Why should I stay?

ROMEO: It would be a pain to recast you, I guess. I would probably have to come to extra rehearsals. That would be super annoying. What's so hard about being Juliet anyway?

JULIET: The lights are bright. They make my eyes water and my face hot. It's kinda uncomfortable.

ROMEO: You get used to the lights.

JULIET: You do?

ROMEO: Probably, yeah.

JULIET: I don't know if I can.

ROMEO: Well try? I guess?

JULIET: Maybe.

ROMEO: Whatever.

(ROMEO exits. End of scene)

Before we stop and analyze the scene above, let's see that same setup but with different stakes:

(JULIET sits on a sofa in the greenroom. ROMEO enters and sits next to her.)

ROMEO: Hey.

JULIET: Hey.

ROMEO: I heard you might quit the show.

JULIET: Oh. You heard about that?

ROMEO: Yeah, the rest of the cast is really freaked out.

JULIET: I didn't mean to put anybody on edge—

ROMEO: We're all working really hard, and we open in just a week and a half—

JULIET: I know! And that's why I haven't just walked out. Everyone is working so hard and I don't want to ruin the production.

ROMEO: Then stick it out! It can't be that bad, you're one of the stars!

JULIET: Well, that's the problem! I have no idea what I'm doing! I should never have even auditioned. Every time I get on that stage I have to fight the urge to run far, far, far away. You'd all be better off without me anyway.

ROMEO: That is not true at all! You wouldn't have been cast if the Director didn't see something in you.

JULIET: You're just saying that.

ROMEO: No, seriously. So many people wanted the lead.

JULIET: I know! That makes it even worse, I'm just the idiotic newbie that doesn't deserve to play Juliet! I'm going to make a fool of myself and get laughed at for the rest of my life!

ROMEO: Hey, you shouldn't talk about yourself like that. And anyway, we were all new to this at one point.

JULIET: It's just. Stressful. Really, really, really stressful.

ROMEO: I get that. I remember my first show, I was so stressed I threw up opening night.

JULIET: You did?

ROMEO: It was a miracle I missed my costume. I had to furiously brush my teeth before my entrance.

JULIET: I can't believe it, you're so good up onstage—

ROMEO: You're so good up there too!

JULIET: You're—you're just saying that so I won't quit.

ROMEO: No, really. You're . . . You have an honesty about you. You don't put on a fake show. You're just you.

JULIET: Well, yeah, who else could I be?

ROMEO: It's hard to be honest onstage. I have to work at it, but it just comes naturally to you. We need that in the play. Don't you want this to be the best production it can be?

JULIET: Yes! I do! I really do.

ROMEO: Then stay. Stay for me. I can help you work on your nerves, if you like. I have some techniques that have really helped me.

JULIET: You'd do that for me?

ROMEO: Absolutely. How about after rehearsal?

JULIET: Okay . . . Yeah. I'll try.

ROMEO: Cool.

(ROMEO exits. End of scene.)

❯ Scene Study ❮

How does the second scene compare to the first? What is at stake in each version? Do you think differently about the characters? How did the change in their stakes affect your investment?

- What are the characters' **objectives** in Scene One and Scene Two?
    - Do they change from the first to the second scene?
- What is at **stake** for the characters in the first scene?
- What is at **stake** for the characters in the second scene?
- Do you feel differently about the characters in the first scene than you do in the second scene?
    - Do you find yourself more invested in one of the scenes?

Writing Cue ❯❯

Now it's your turn to play around with stakes! You'll write a two-character scene, identifying what is at stake for each of the characters before you start. As always, you can flip back to your lists for inspiration, or rewrite one of the scenes above in your own words.

For this exercise, you will need:

- Two characters.
- Each with their own **objectives**.
- Both characters will take **actions** in order to achieve their **objectives**.
- Before you start, you will identify exactly what is at **stake** for each of your characters. What will happen if they succeed? What will happen if they fail?
    - The characters can have a shared **objective**, with **stakes** that will affect them both if they fail, OR they can have opposing **objectives**, where their success is dependent on the other's failure.

Set your timer for five minutes at least. Ready? GO!

❮ Interval ❯

- Once the timer sounds, stop writing!
- Stand, stretch, move, shake it out.
- How did that feel?
    - Was anything surprising?
    - Was anything harder than you expected? Easier than expected?
- Read your scene out loud, or if you're in a group, have volunteers share.
    - What did each character want?
    - What was at **stake** for them?

THROUGH-THE-ROOF STAKES SCENE

When playing with stakes, sometimes the bigger the stakes, the easier they are to understand. We've done low stakes, we've done stakes that felt natural to the characters' objectives, but what if we turn those stakes up even more? Let's see!

(JULIET sits on a sofa in the greenroom. ROMEO enters and sits next to her.)

ROMEO: Juliet! Thank goodness you're here!

JULIET: Not for long, I was about to leave—

ROMEO: Are you quitting the show?

JULIET: I am, I have to.

ROMEO: NO! You can't!

JULIET: I don't want to hurt you, or anyone here, but I have to! I have to quit!

ROMEO: You don't understand, if you quit, if you walk away from this play, I won't survive.

JULIET: You . . . wouldn't . . . survive? What do you mean?

ROMEO: Exactly what it sounds like, if you quit this production, I will die.

JULIET: Die? Like, dead die?

ROMEO: Yes. Exactly. Dead die. I just found out. I have a rare disease that means my body cannot tolerate a castmate quitting a production.

JULIET: That's horrible!

ROMEO: I know!

JULIET: But you don't understand, I HAVE to quit!

ROMEO: Does my life mean nothing to you?

JULIET: It means everything to me! Of course it does! It's only . . . I also have a rare disease, you see. If I *stay* in this production I will die!

ROMEO: Like dead, die?

JULIET: Exactly!

ROMEO: NOOOOOOO!

JULIET: I KNOW!

ROMEO: So that means . . .

JULIET: Only one of us will live!

ROMEO: One of us will have to sacrifice the other!

JULIET: I never should have auditioned for this play! I just wanted to be a tree!

ROMEO: Curse you, rare theatrical diseases, CURSE YOU!

(ROMEO and JULIET both sob. End of scene.)

Scene Study

- What is at **stake** for the characters in this version of the scene?
- Compare these **stakes** to those in "Playing with Stakes: Scenes One and Two."
    - How do these new **stakes** change the characters' **actions**?
- How do the **stakes** in this version change your reaction to the characters?
    - To the scene?

Writing Cue ➤➤

I'm about to make you get as silly as I did in the scene above! You are welcome.

For this exercise, I want you to take the scene that you wrote earlier and turn the stakes up to an eleven. That means, if a life was on the line, now an entire family's lives are in danger. If a school was in danger, now the whole city is! The world was at stake? Well now the universe is. The bottom line: go BIG BIG BIG with the stakes this go-around. Don't be afraid of the silly, it's almost impossible for this not to be silly.

In this exercise, you will need:

- The scene you wrote earlier that had:
    - Two characters.
    - Both with their own **objectives**.
    - Both characters will take **actions** in order to achieve their **objectives**.
- Before you start, you will identify exactly what is at **stake** for each of your characters. What will happen if they succeed? What will happen if they fail?
    - The characters can have a shared **objective**, with **stakes** that will affect them both if they fail, OR they can have opposing **objectives**, where their success is dependent on the other's failure.
- Turn the **stakes** way up! At least double what's on the line, but feel free to go bigger.
- Embrace the silly!

Get your timer ready! Give yourself at least five minutes, but at this point feel free to have the minimum jump up to ten minutes. All set? GO!

❮ Interval ❯

- Once the timer sounds, stop writing!
- Stand, stretch, move, shake it out.
- How did that feel?
    - Was anything surprising?
    - Was anything harder than you expected? Easier than expected?
- Read your own scene out loud, playing both characters, or if you're in a group, have volunteers share.
    - Compare the **stakes** in these scenes to the **stakes** in the original.
        - How do the new **stakes** change the characters?
        - How do the new **stakes** change the **actions** of the characters?
        - How do the new **stakes** impact you as an audience member as you read your own scene out loud?

SPOTLIGHT ON STAKES

Ever been to a scene night? When I first started writing, I had two groups I regularly frequented, where for five or ten bucks, you'd get to hear ten pages of your writing read out loud by local actors. It's a great way to meet people, hear your work, and get feedback from actors and your fellow playwrights. Sometimes I'd bring in ten pages and they would just fall flat. No one would lean in, the mere ten pages would feel more like twenty, and absolutely no one would laugh. It took me a long time to realize it, but each and every time that happened, it was because I hadn't set the stakes high enough for my characters. While you're working away at these exercises, and later when you dive into writing plays, remember the magic lever stakes can be.

There's nothing wrong with erring on the side of "big" as far as stakes are concerned, especially as you are still figuring all this out. Big stakes allow for you to see each of the tools at their most vibrant, as big stakes often demand big objectives and big action. Later, as you're fully in the water and swimming laps with ease, you can set your stakes to whatever level gives your work the balance you hope to achieve.

CONFLICT

MUCH LIKE **STAKES**, where something has to be on the line for our characters, our characters also need **conflict**: something or someone that pushes back against them. Without **conflict**, our protagonists wouldn't need to use **action** to reach their **objective**—they could just walk up and get what they want. And that would make for a very short play.

Conflict is the fuel for dramatic writing. The bread and butter. Just like we did with objective, action, and stakes, we can find conflict out in the wild. In fact, it's there every time objectives don't align.

Take two coworkers that each have a different idea of how to tackle a project. Their objective is to have their idea used when moving forward. Their actions could be arguing, pleading, manipulating, bribing, or undermining the other. Their stakes could be a promotion, or pride, or self-worth. These coworkers, with their different plans of action, act as one another's conflict.

Or, take me and my two high-intensity dogs heading into a dog park. My objective is to walk two polite and well-behaved dogs into the park. I imagine their objective is to GET THERE, NOW, RIGHT NOW, GET THERE, QUICKER, GET THERE, NOW, GET THERE, GET THERE NOW! My stakes in the situation are both physical—they're about to pull my arms out of their sockets—and social—my pride in being a responsible dog owner. Their stakes, I imagine, are WE CANNOT WASTE ONE INSTANT OF THE FUN AND THE RUNNING AND ALL THE DOG FRIENDS. And so my dogs and I, just like the coworkers, are in conflict with one another. We cannot both have our objectives, and we will remain in conflict until one of us achieves our goal. In the case of me and my dogs, my dogs always win and bark in their nervous joy to their hearts' content.

THE RANGE OF CONFLICT

On the surface it can feel like conflict has to be a screaming match, but that isn't the case. For example, if the conflict is that you want to leave my house and I don't want you to go (our objectives clash), you might keep looking at your watch, while I offer you a snack. It's important to realize conflict's range, because otherwise all of our characters would be yelling at one another all the time, which would get old fast.

We learn about our characters and their relationships through conflict. Different people handle conflict in a multitude of ways, and our characters should be no different. Even more variety is introduced when you consider the specific relationship in which the conflict arises. For example, if conflict pops up over where a group goes to lunch, that probably looks very different with a group of friends than a group of coworkers. We handle conflict with strangers differently than we do with loved ones, and usually we have a specific way for each of our specific loved ones as well.

DIRECT AND INNER CONFLICT

We're going to explore two different types of **conflict** in this chapter: **direct conflict** and **inner conflict**. **Direct conflict** occurs between two characters. These characters each have an objective and that objective is at odds with the other character's objective. For example:

- Grandma wants to spend Christmas at the beach while Grandpa wants to go to the desert.
- Ben wants to turn in the duffle bag stuffed with over fifty grand they found in the park to the proper authorities while his best friend wants to keep it.

Two characters. Two objectives. One must fail for the other to succeed.

Inner conflict happens within a single character. One way to think about it is when our **want** and our **need** is in conflict. Yes, we all want things, but we need things too. For example, we need to eat in order to live. We need water. We need air. Needs are necessary, wants don't have to be. Often our needs and wants are on the same page. If you're cast in a play and you want to do well, you will need to memorize your lines. But need and want don't always see eye to eye, and when they don't, you get **inner conflict**. Here are a few simple examples of needs and wants being in conflict:

- I **need** to do the dishes, but I **want** to watch TV.
- I **need** eight hours of sleep, but I **want** to finish this book.
- I **need** to buy groceries with the last of my paycheck, but I **want** to buy the twenty-foot-tall skeleton from Home Depot.

FIND THE CONFLICT

Think back to your favorite books, movies, plays, and TV shows. What examples of conflict come to mind? Are these examples of direct or inner conflict? Push yourself and try to find an example in which the conflict is humorous. One that turns to physicality. One that is brutal. One that is loving.

- Think of examples of **conflict**.
    - How would you categorize each?
- Push yourself to find at least five examples that are contrary to what most people typically think of when they hear the word **conflict**.

DIRECT CONFLICT SCENE

Let's head back to that production of *Romeo and Juliet* to see an example of direct conflict.

(SET DESIGNER and LIGHTING DESIGNER are onstage. They paint a wall, adding details to make it look like a castle wall.)

SET DESIGNER: Nice ivy detail.

LIGHTING DESIGNER: Thanks. Letting the muse direct me.

SET DESIGNER: Won't be too much longer, maybe we'll get out of here before midnight tonight.

LIGHTING DESIGNER: Speak for yourself, once I'm done helping you paint, I have to check the levels on the lights against all these new details.

SET DESIGNER: Oh dang, I hadn't realized. If you need to head up to the booth—

LIGHTING DESIGNER: No, I want to test against the finished backdrop. And anyway, I kinda love painting. Maybe in another life I did sets.

SET DESIGNER: Well I need to do something for you, you're really doing me a solid.

LIGHTING DESIGNER: Buy me dinner, then we'll call it even.

SET DESIGNER: Deal. I'll order now, I can feel the beginnings of a grumbling tummy anyway.

LIGHTING DESIGNER: Perfect, I'm starving.

SET DESIGNER: What do you like on your pizza? I'm a big meat eater, but I can go veg if you don't do animals.

LIGHTING DESIGNER: Actually, I'm kinda burnt out on pizza.

SET DESIGNER: Oh. Really? Is that possible?

LIGHTING DESIGNER: It's all we eat!

SET DESIGNER: Yeah, because it's amazing.

LIGHTING DESIGNER: Can you just get some Chinese? The Golden Dragon delivers.

SET DESIGNER: Chinese?

LIGHTING DESIGNER: They have this spicy chicken that's super tasty—

SET DESIGNER: Well, if it's chicken you're after, the pizza place does this barbecue chicken pizza—

LIGHTING DESIGNER: Chicken and barbecue sauce on pizza? That's a horror story.

SET DESIGNER: We can get the sauce on the side.

LIGHTING DESIGNER: I just don't feel like pizza.

SET DESIGNER: Right. You said. But, I don't know, I am paying . . .

LIGHTING DESIGNER: Yeah, because I am helping you out with painting!

SET DESIGNER: But you're also helping yourself out.

LIGHTING DESIGNER: How do you figure?

SET DESIGNER: Well you said you can't really check the lights until the back wall of the set is finished being painted. If you don't help me, it'll take me twice as long, and you'll be stuck here most of the night.

LIGHTING DESIGNER: True, but I could always get a nap on the greenroom couch and just wait until you're done.

SET DESIGNER: Prop Master is already passed out on the couch.

LIGHTING DESIGNER: Okay, not the couch, but I could find a corner and catch up on some Z's.

SET DESIGNER: You could. But you won't. Face it, you like action. You want to be in the middle of everything.

LIGHTING DESIGNER: Well maybe I could take my active self to costumes and help with some sewing. I bet you they'd get me some Chinese food.

SET DESIGNER: Deserter!

LIGHTING DESIGNER: What's your problem with Chinese food anyway?

SET DESIGNER: I don't hate Chinese food.

LIGHTING DESIGNER: You just don't want to eat it?

SET DESIGNER: Maybe if it was more flat and circular with cheese and tomato sauce . . .

LIGHTING DESIGNER: So your problem with Chinese food is that it isn't pizza?

SET DESIGNER: Yes! Exactly! So glad you get it!

LIGHTING DESIGNER: You can't just order both?

SET DESIGNER: Order both what?

LIGHTING DESIGNER: Chinese and pizza?

SET DESIGNER: Whoa, you think I'm made out of money? But if you want Chinese so bad, I guess I can take one for the team and eat an entire pizza . . .

LIGHTING DESIGNER: I'm broke until opening. It's like half the reason I'm being so helpful, it makes it more likely that others will feed me.

SET DESIGNER: Beggars can't be choosers then, maybe?

LIGHTING DESIGNER: I just can't eat pizza again. It's like the fifth time this week! Have some sympathy!

SET DESIGNER: You're really going to stop me from having the perfect pizza week? I'm just a few days shy of all pizza all the time!

LIGHTING DESIGNER: You'd marry pizza if given the chance.

SET DESIGNER: Oh definitely, no hesitation.

LIGHTING DESIGNER: So there's nothing I can do to convince you to get Chinese?

SET DESIGNER: You put up a brave fight, but I'm going to go with . . . no.

(SET DESIGNER orders. End of scene.)

Scene Study

- What is each character's **objective**?
- What **actions** do the characters take in order to achieve their **objective**?
- What is the **conflict**?
- Is there any common ground between the characters?
    - If so, what is it?

Writing Cue >>

Writing time! We will be writing a scene where two characters are in direct conflict with each other. To start let's brainstorm a list of potential **direct conflicts** between characters.

Put two minutes on your timer! Remember to keep those hands working until your timer goes off. Ready? GO!

Examples:

- Food! Obviously a go-to of mine. But it is a situation where we've most likely all been. After all, who hasn't had a "what will we eat now?" conversation?
- Where should we go on vacation?
- Should we fix the house or buy a fancy new car with that unexpected money?

Time to write your scene! Use one of your just-brainstormed direct conflict situations, or steal and rewrite the scene from above. In this scene, you will need:

- Two characters.
- Each of whom have **objectives**.
    - These **objectives** are in **direct conflict** with one another, meaning one has to fail for the other to succeed.
- Each character uses **action** to get what they want.
- Something at **stake** for each of the characters, meaning they gain or lose something as a result of their success or failure with their respective **objectives**.

Put at least ten minutes on a timer, and don't stop until the timer sounds. We're focusing on **direct conflict**. Ready? GO!

❮ Interval ❯

- Once the timer sounds, stop writing!
- Stand, stretch, move, shake it out.
- How did that feel?
    - Was anything surprising?
    - Was anything harder than you expected? Easier than expected?
- Read your own scene out loud, or if you're working in a group, have volunteers share.
    - What did each character **want**?
    - How did these **wants/objectives conflict**?
    - What **action** was each taking? Can you put it into **active** words?
    - How would you describe the **conflict**?
    - Did someone win? Did someone lose? Did they both win or both lose?

INNER CONFLICT SCENE

Now we'll see an example of inner conflict in a scene.

(SOUND DESIGNER and TYBALT sit in the sound booth. SOUND DESIGNER hits a button and dinosaur sounds start to play. They listen. Once the dino sounds end:)

SOUND DESIGNER: Perfect, right?

TYBALT: I'm sorry, perfect for what?

SOUND DESIGNER: Isn't it obvious? The fight scene.

TYBALT: The fight scene?

SOUND DESIGNER: When Romeo kills you.

TYBALT: That was a dinosaur, wasn't it?

SOUND DESIGNER: Velociraptor to be exact.

TYBALT: That's the cue that will play as Romeo and I fight?

SOUND DESIGNER: Right, exactly! I knew you would get it! Earlier, when you kill Mercutio, I'm gonna play big cat noises. Because you're the Prince of Cats! My theme is inner beasts, you know?

TYBALT: Um. I'm not sure I totally get it.

SOUND DESIGNER: When you're dueling with your swords and stuff, these sounds will be going on. Like, instead of clanging swords.

TYBALT: But we're using swords!

SOUND DESIGNER: Right, but that would be so boring and obvious.

TYBALT: And the Director just approved those sounds?

SOUND DESIGNER: Not exactly. I guess their "vision" is a clean and classical take on the text. SO BORING.

TYBALT: I don't know about boring, remember there are duels and swords and poison and—

SOUND DESIGNER: MASSIVE YAWN. I think the set should be a concrete background with like graffiti, and the Capulets should be aliens from another planet, and the Montagues should all be like ancient earth beasts. Like the giant sloth! And the saber-toothed tiger!

TYBALT: And velociraptors?

SOUND DESIGNER: YES! It'd be SO COOL, right? I can see it all so clearly and it is SO RAD, but the Director just won't listen!

TYBALT: So you're just going to play the sounds anyway?

SOUND DESIGNER: I *want* to. I want to so bad! But the Director said I'd be FIRED if I did that. And I'm afraid if I get fired from this production they won't bring me back in the spring for *Godzilla: The Musical.*

TYBALT: So just play sword noises, or whatever the Director is asking for!

SOUND DESIGNER: I know I should! I get that. Totally. 100 percent understand that the smart thing to do, the safe bet, would be to just play the regular noises audiences expect from *Romeo and Juliet.* Lute music. Rapiers whining through the air. Wind, I guess. Blah blah boring.

TYBALT: But isn't your job to support the Director's vision? Not your own?

SOUND DESIGNER: Whoa. Whose side are you on?

TYBALT: I'm on the side of you not getting fired! And the play's side! I have lines during those fight scenes! Important lines!

SOUND DESIGNER: But this way the audience will have to listen *harder*, lean in and all that.

TYBALT: How are you the same designer that made everyone cry with that soft piano music at the end of *'night Mother*?

SOUND DESIGNER: I just want to show that I have range!

TYBALT: Wild beast range?

SOUND DESIGNER: Everyone would talk about it! For a long, long time!

TYBALT: Not in a good way though! Look, just, and I'm saying this as a friend, and as an actor who doesn't want to be embarrassed onstage, just do what the Director wants.

SOUND DESIGNER: UGH. I should. I probably very much should . . . But I *want* the velociraptor. I *want* the saber-toothed tiger! What did giant sloths even sound like? I should research—

TYBALT: No, no you shouldn't.

SOUND DESIGNER: I don't know what I'll do. It is SUCH a hard choice! On the one hand is my creative intuition, the other my duty as a sound designer. It's a pickle. A real pickle. Let's just listen one more time. Yeah, that'll help. And *really* listen, okay? Listen and *visualize.*

(SOUND DESIGNER plays the dino sounds again for TYBALT. End of scene.)

➤ Scene Study ❮

- What is Tybalt's **objective**?
- What is the Sound Designer's **objective**?
- Which character is experiencing **inner conflict**?
    - What is that character's **need**?
    - What is that character's **want**?

Writing Cue ➤➤

Now it's your turn! First let's brainstorm some examples of **inner conflict** to give you options in your scene. Put two minutes on a timer, don't stop until the timer goes off. Ready? GO!

Examples of inner conflict:

- A special family dinner is scheduled on a night you'd planned to see a concert.
- You're on a budget and have everything at home to make dinner, but a delivered pizza would be oh-so delicious.
- You found an affordable apartment, but there's another one that's twice as expensive and much prettier.

Armed with your brainstormed list, let's get to the inner conflict scene. Your scene should include:

- Two characters.
- Both of whom have **objectives**.
- Both of whom use **action** to reach those **objectives**.
- There is something at **stake** for both characters.
- At least one of your characters experiences **inner conflict** where their **need** and **want** oppose one another.

Set a timer for ten minutes. Ready? GO!

❮ Interval ❯

- Once the timer sounds, stop writing!
- Stand, stretch, move, shake it out.
- How did that feel?
    - Was anything surprising?
    - Was anything harder than you expected? Easier than expected?

- Read your own scene out loud, playing both characters, or if you're in a group, have volunteers share their scenes:
    - Which character has **inner conflict**?
        - What is the **conflict**?
        - What is the **want**?
        - What is the **need**?

SPOTLIGHT ON CONFLICT

Understanding how to play with **conflict** in your writing helps you explore your characters and their relationships. Conflict as a tool has a wide range, from knockdown brawls to polite disagreements, and many situations in between. Conflict occurs whenever characters' objectives are at odds. How your characters handle this clash shows the audience who they are, and who they choose to be with the other characters onstage. Direct conflict is between at least two characters, whereas inner conflict happens within a single character. Conflict can also show the audience how much your characters' objective means to them, and how much is at stake.

My play *The Red House Monster* leads its hero, Hannah, to confront an evil monster, just as her father did before her. When she finally is face to face with said monster, she gets a vastly different conflict than what she expected. Instead of the classic conflict of good versus evil, she is confronted with a lonely and misunderstood aging loner, and the conflict becomes inner conflict. After all, if this monster isn't a monster at all, is she a hero? Was her beloved father? And what if the town discovered the truth? But heroes don't attack unprovoked . . . The two sides of Hannah's inner conflict are well-matched, and put her in a position to make an impossible decision. And that's good. At least for storytelling. We want things to be hard for our characters. We want conflict, adversity. Just as we think of conflict as something that builds character in real life, conflict for our characters gives them depth and complexity in a play. So put them through the wringer! Bake conflict into every fold of your play, and then explore that range. When is conflict handled with love? With a joke? With harsh words? Pit characters against one another, pit characters against themselves. Make it difficult. Make it impossible. See where they rise to the occasion, and where they fail. The harder you make it, the more your audience will lean in, eager to see where the story goes.

OBSTACLE

OBSTACLES OBSTRUCT PATHWAYS and make it harder for your character to get what they want. Why do we make it so hard? It makes a character more active, which keeps your audience engaged. We love to watch struggle. It's another example of the stage reflecting life. Audiences want to see your characters work. Without anything in their way, it would be too easy.

A BOULDER IN YOUR PATH

Obstacles and **conflict** have a lot in common. Both make life complicated for characters, forcing them to work. The difference between the two is that conflict includes elements that may change, while obstacles include facts that won't change. For example, you're on a hike with an objective to reach the mountain's peak, and as you're going along, you meet a giant boulder blocking the hiking trail. That, my friends, is an obstacle. You can climb over it, but the boulder remains right in its place on the trail.

Not all obstacles are **physical obstacles**. Characters are often plagued by **non-physical obstacles**. Like their physical counterpoints, **non-physical obstacles** are not things you can negotiate with or change. They are facts that if they do somehow change, they do so without input from characters. Non-physical obstacles can be thought of as rules your characters have been depending on, and when they radically change, they cannot be changed back. Non-physical obstacles could be an empty bank account or rejection from a dream university. They aren't a physical impairment, but they stop our characters in their tracks and force them to figure out a new path or turn back all together.

FIND THE OBSTACLE

Let's think back to our favorite stories, whether they're books, plays, movies, or TV shows. What are some examples of obstacles that come to mind?

- Start a list of **physical obstacles** and another list of **non-physical obstacles.**
  - How did those **obstacles** change the stories? The characters?
  - What happened to the **stakes** after those **obstacles** were presented?
  - What about the characters' **actions**?

Stay on the lookout for both types of obstacles when you're watching or reading or listening to stories. What type of obstacle is it? How does it affect the characters?

PHYSICAL OBSTACLE SCENE

A fallen tree across the road. A huge, gaping hole that just tore open your front yard during an earthquake. These are examples of physical obstacles. Unlike with conflict, there's no amount of talking that can change them—with physical obstacles, a new game plan is needed. Let's go back to *Romeo and Juliet* to see an example of a physical obstacle.

(The greenroom. A giant fruit basket sits square in the middle. Now, when I say "giant," I mean GIANT. Like well over fifteen feet tall, giant. It's the Home Depot skeleton of fruit baskets. It should confound logic how this fruit basket even got into this room. The fruit basket completely blocks movement from one side of the room to the other. LADY CAPULET stares open-mouthed at the basket.)

LADY CAPULET: . . . WHAT the—

(PROP MASTER enters from the other side of the room, the two talk to one another through the open weave of the basket.)

PROP MASTER: Whoa. What is . . . Is that a fruit basket?

LADY CAPULET: I guess it's the *Land of the Lost* fruit basket . . . How did they even get it IN here?

PROP MASTER: It is so big!

LADY CAPULET: I don't think BIG even begins to cover the size of this fruit basket.

PROP MASTER: Oh no. Oh no, no, no, no, no.

LADY CAPULET: Did you do this? On purpose?

PROP MASTER: Not exactly.

LADY CAPULET: And what, you just forgot it in here?

PROP MASTER: No! I would never, I mean how could you forget . . . I'll never forget this basket for as long as I live! No. I ordered it.

LADY CAPULET: You ordered it?

PROP MASTER: Yeah. I ordered it.

LADY CAPULET: Where do you order a twenty-foot-tall basket?

PROP MASTER: I think it's only seventeen feet.

LADY CAPULET: Oh, so sorry I got the measurements wrong on your ginormous basket!

PROP MASTER: No, it's just, I thought I was getting a seventeen-*inch* basket.

LADY CAPULET: A seventeen-inch basket would make sense.

PROP MASTER: Yes! And that's what I thought I was getting.

LADY CAPULET: Seems like you were wrong.

PROP MASTER: Oh so very wrong.

LADY CAPULET: What scene is the fruit basket even for?

PROP MASTER: The party scene. You're setting them out—

LADY CAPULET: *I* am setting this out?

PROP MASTER: For your guests, for the party. You're setting them out, and you go up to Juliet's room to see if she's ready, and it's in your arms—you forgot you were carrying it, you know? And then we see them later, during the party scene, decorating the tables.

LADY CAPULET: I am not going to be able to carry that.

PROP MASTER: No, obviously.

LADY CAPULET: How did you even accidentally order a seventeen-foot basket instead of a seventeen-inch basket?

PROP MASTER: I guess I didn't read the fine print. I didn't even order it, not really. It was listed online for free as long as they could drop them off by today.

LADY CAPULET: Right, they probably wanted their house back.

PROP MASTER: Wow, it is so big! I wonder if we can somehow make this work? Obviously you wouldn't carry it around, but maybe somewhere . . .

LADY CAPULET: I'm actually more concerned about how I can get it out of my way. I came in here for the bathroom.

PROP MASTER: Oh, tough timing! Um, let's see, it probably isn't that heavy. It must be hollow, right? If I just nudge it a bit you should be able to wiggle around . . .

(PROP MASTER starts with a little nudge on the fruit basket. It doesn't budge. PROP MASTER pushes. Nothing. PROP MASTER bends over and pushes with all of their might. Absolutely no movement on the giant fruit basket.)

PROP MASTER: It won't budge!

LADY CAPULET: I can see that!

PROP MASTER: Maybe if we try together? You push and I'll pull.

(PROP MASTER and LADY CAPULET try to move the giant fruit basket together. Nothing.)

LADY CAPULET: I am going to pee my pants!

PROP MASTER: Just go around, through the theater door, the way I came in.

LADY CAPULET: Ugh! Okay! If I have an accident I am blaming it on you!

(LADY CAPULET exits. PROP MASTER tries again to move the basket with no luck. LADY CAPULET enters.)

LADY CAPULET: There are more!

PROP MASTER: More what?

LADY CAPULET: More baskets! I'm blocked in! The other one is just on the other side of this door. How many of these did you get?

PROP MASTER: Look, half a dozen fruit baskets is totally normal for a big party.

LADY CAPULET: HALF A DOZEN?

PROP MASTER: The Capulets are super fancy and rich!

LADY CAPULET: But there are HALF A DOZEN of these SEVENTEEN-FOOT-TALL fruit baskets in the theater?

PROP MASTER: I can understand why they wanted to get rid of them so bad. They really do take up a lot of space, and they're so heavy. What are they even made out of?

LADY CAPULET: FOCUS! I need to PEE! HELP ME!

PROP MASTER: Right, right! Okay. I think you're going to have to climb up.

LADY CAPULET: I'm not climbing the giant fruit basket!

PROP MASTER: Then find a cup over there, I guess?

LADY CAPULET: I AM NOT PEEING IN A CUP!

PROP MASTER: Then you're going to have to climb!

LADY CAPULET: Climbing is very out of character for Lady Capulet, I hope you realize that.

PROP MASTER: Is it more out of character than peeing in a cup?

LADY CAPULET: Fine. FINE! But if I break my neck, I'm holding you personally responsible.

PROP MASTER: Grab on to the banana! Then use the weave like a ladder!

LADY CAPULET: Yes! Obviously!

(LADY CAPULET climbs the giant fruit basket.)

PROP MASTER: Good! Now grab onto the orange and boost yourself up. Careful with that pear, it doesn't look completely secured to the rest of the basket. Okay, I think you're over the hardest part, now just use the grapes as steps to get down. I'm spotting you.

(LADY CAPULET is at the top, she starts the climb down.)

LADY CAPULET: If you ever tell anyone about this, I will murder you.

PROP MASTER: I get that. Completely.

(LADY CAPULET reaches the other side.)

LADY CAPULET: Thanks for your help. I still hold you responsible for this mess.

PROP MASTER: As do I.

(LADY CAPULET heads for the bathroom door.)

LADY CAPULET: I'll help you find the others! After I'm done! Before the Director finds them and completely blows a gasket!

(LADY CAPULET exits into the bathroom. PROP MASTER yells after her.)

PROP MASTER: THANK YOU! . . . Oh. I'm so getting fired over this.

(End of scene.)

Scene Study

- What was the **physical obstacle** in the scene?
- How did the **physical obstacle** hamper one or both of the characters from reaching their **objectives**?
- How did the **physical obstacle** influence the **actions** of the characters?

Writing Cue ››

It's time to write your own physical obstacle scene! Feel free to flip back to your **brainstorming** list of items you'd be hard pressed to hold in your hand, or take two minutes and come up with a fresh new list of potential physical obstacles. For this exercise, you will need:

- Two characters, both of whom have an **objective**.
- Both use **action** to work toward their **objective**.
- A **physical obstacle** that is in the way of one or both of your characters.
- Feel free to steal the setup and characters from above and write your own version of it!

Get your timer ready! Give yourself ten minutes, but feel free to bump up to fifteen. Ready? GO!

If you're feeling stuck:

- Don't let overthinking get in your way! Remember, I used a giant fruit basket. I double-dog dare you to get sillier than that.
- Let the **obstacle** make your characters more **active**. Make them work!
- Let the **obstacle** raise the **stakes**! Make your characters really want their **objective**!

❮ Interval ❯

- Once the timer sounds, stop writing!
- Stand, stretch, move, shake it out.
- How did that feel?
  - Was anything surprising?
  - Was anything harder than you expected? Easier than expected?
- Read your own scene out loud, playing both characters. Or, if you're in a group, ask for volunteers to share.
  - What was the **physical obstacle**?
  - How did it affect the characters' **objectives** and **actions**?
  - How did it affect the **stakes** in the scene?

NON-PHYSICAL OBSTACLE SCENE

Much like a physical obstacle, non-physical obstacles aren't something to be negotiated with. They're unavoidable. Like I mentioned before, a rule your characters have been depending on has just radically changed and cannot be changed back. The same can be said for physical obstacles; after all, that seventeen-foot-tall fruit basket from the previous section certainly changed the rules of the greenroom for both the Prop Master and Lady Capulet. Let's head back to *Romeo and Juliet* to see a non-physical obstacle example:

(STAGE MANAGER and DIRECTOR are in the house of the theater.)

STAGE MANAGER: Oh I caught you, good! We need to chat about—

DIRECTOR: Oh yes we need to chat! We need to have a good long chat! We need an emergency production meeting this afternoon. Right after rehearsal. Nothing is right! Juliet's dress for the party scene needs to be fancier. I want her dripping in riches, same with Lady Capulet! I want thunder and lightning for the duels, and rain! I want them fighting in the rain! And wind if we can get it. The storm represents the storm within the characters, the turmoil from this family feud. And I want live rabbits onstage when Romeo calls up to Juliet's balcony. I don't know which designer that would fall under, but they can figure that out amongst themselves. I want fireworks, and not projections, actual fireworks—

STAGE MANAGER: Hold on. Real fireworks? I don't think we can set off real fireworks inside.

DIRECTOR: I don't care what we CAN or CAN'T do! This is theatre! Just let me have it!

STAGE MANAGER: And rain. And wind. AND more opulent costumes. Bunnies?

DIRECTOR: I need rabbits, I never said a word about bunnies.

STAGE MANAGER: We're already over budget. That's what I was trying to tell you.

DIRECTOR: Why does that have anything to do with me?

STAGE MANAGER: I know this is your first time directing—

DIRECTOR: Do NOT belittle me!

STAGE MANAGER: I'm not belittling anyone. I'm just saying, part of your job is keeping everything within budget.

DIRECTOR: I have vision! I have dreams!

STAGE MANAGER: And that costs money. Of which we are out.

DIRECTOR: I thought it was the designers' jobs to stay within their own budgets! Didn't you tell them their spending limits?

STAGE MANAGER: I did, but you keep approving everyone to go over their budgets! And then you don't even tell me about it!

DIRECTOR: I would tell you, but you bring such a negative energy to everything.

STAGE MANAGER: We want to produce your vision of the play, but you have GOT to stop overspending. You can't buy anything new. Or if you do, the designers will have to return something they already bought.

DIRECTOR: No! I need it all! I need it all or nothing!

STAGE MANAGER: Then you are very close to getting nothing.

DIRECTOR: Is that a threat? Are you trying to usurp me? ME?

STAGE MANAGER: It wasn't a threat. It's just the facts.

DIRECTOR: You've been eyeing my job since day one! Don't think I didn't notice! I have eyes and ears all over this theater!

STAGE MANAGER: You mean the Assistant Stage Manager you're making spy on the rest of us?

DIRECTOR: . . . I . . . No . . . Not at all . . . I would never.

STAGE MANAGER: Look pal, just get your budget under control.

DIRECTOR: And if I refuse?

STAGE MANAGER: I don't know, they cancel the production and we all get fired?

DIRECTOR: That is unacceptable! This is my directing debut!

STAGE MANAGER: Right, and a lot of people have put a lot of work into this.

DIRECTOR: Just ask the producer to raise the budget, won't you?

STAGE MANAGER: No. I won't. I can't. They won't budge. You are out of money. You have to make what you already have work.

DIRECTOR: But I want rabbits! And a storm! And more! So so so much more!

STAGE MANAGER: Well that's not gonna happen, so get used to it.

DIRECTOR: Please?

STAGE MANAGER: No.

DIRECTOR: Please, please, please, *please*?

STAGE MANAGER: Still no.

DIRECTOR: But what if we worked out an agreement?

STAGE MANAGER: Like what, you fund the show?

DIRECTOR: Not that, I have no money. Like, we just keep spending and you agree to look the other way?

STAGE MANAGER: Absolutely no.

DIRECTOR: I'll be your best friend!

STAGE MANAGER: Pass.

DIRECTOR: It is very negative. Your energy.

STAGE MANAGER: Look, I've seen directors pull off more with less. Trust me when I say we already have everything we need for a great show!

DIRECTOR: But it doesn't look exactly like it does in my head!

STAGE MANAGER: That's not possible!

DIRECTOR: I will not compromise!

(STAGE MANAGER's walkie-talkie beeps, they hold it to their mouth.)

STAGE MANAGER: Go for Stage Manager . . . Okay, calm down. Just relax. I'm coming to help, okay?

DIRECTOR: Did we get a sudden and unexpected giant donation?

STAGE MANAGER: No. Of course we didn't. Apparently there's some problem in the greenroom. Props needs me.

DIRECTOR: Just a little storm? Think about it. Just a very little tiny atmospheric rain and wind and—

STAGE MANAGER: NO!

(STAGE MANAGER exits. DIRECTOR crumples to the floor. End of scene.)

Scene Study

- What were the characters' **objectives**?
- What was the **non-physical obstacle**?
- Did the **non-physical obstacle** impact both characters, or just one?
- Did anyone get what they wanted in the scene?

Writing Cue ❯❯

Before we jump into the non-physical obstacle exercise, let's brainstorm **non-physical obstacles.** What troubles can you throw in your character's way? Get your timer ready with two minutes. Ready? GO!

Examples:

- Budget restrictions, like the example above
- Not enough time in the day
- Not enough experience or knowledge

Great! Now that you have lots of non-physical obstacle options, let's get to your scene! For your non-physical obstacle scene, you will need:

- Two characters.
- Both of whom have an **objective**.
- Both of whom use **action** to achieve their **objective**.
- A **non-physical obstacle** that is in the way of one or both of your characters reaching their **objectives**.
- As always, you have the option to steal the setup and characters from above and write your own version of it.

Get your timer ready! Give yourself ten to fifteen minutes. Ready? GO!

If you're feeling stuck:

- What happens if your **non-physical obstacle** is bigger? Don't be afraid to really make your characters work.

- Focus on **objective**, what do your characters **want**? How does this **non-physical obstacle** impact that?

❮ Interval ❯

- Once the timer sounds, stop writing!
- Stand, stretch, move, shake it out.
- How did that feel?
    - Was anything surprising?
    - Was anything harder than you expected? Easier than expected?
- Read your own scene out loud, playing both characters. Or, if you're in a group, have volunteers share their work.
    - What were the characters' **objectives**?
    - What was the **non-physical obstacle** in their way? Did it impact both characters or just one?
    - What **actions** did the characters take to try and get around the **obstacle**?
    - Did they succeed?

SPOTLIGHT ON OBSTACLE

It might feel like we're torturing our characters, throwing everything—maybe even including the kitchen sink—at them, as they move toward their objective. And that's because we are. In my play *The Book Women*, Erma, one of the librarians delivering books on horseback in rural Kentucky, is met with one of the most unflinching obstacles possible: death. Erma's horse dies while she's in the middle of her route forcing her to change her action in order to achieve her objective.

When I said writing is hard, I didn't just mean for the writer. We torture our characters because if they could just waltz in and achieve their objective that would make for a very short and very uncompelling story.

TACTICS

THE FINAL FUNDAMENTAL TOOL for your playwright toolbox is **tactics**. Another thing I've stolen from my acting background. **Action** shows what our characters **want**, as we see them taking **action** in order to achieve their **objective**. Action makes our audiences lean in, as we love to see active characters onstage. Tactics and action are directly related, as **tactics** are multiple actions that our characters employ as they work away at their objective. We naturally use tactics in everyday life. We can often sense when one action isn't working, and without much thought we will often switch gears and try a new action as we work toward our objective. And like with everything else we've touched on, if it's happening in real life, we want to see that reflected onstage. Using tactics also lays the groundwork for the future actors that will one day pick up your scripts and take your characters into three dimensions.

THE LAST SLICE OF PIZZA

Imagine you're invited to the best kind of party, a party in which there will be pizza. You get to the party a little late, and by then there is but ONE (gasp) slice left. You make a beeline for the box, but a friend picks up this final slice before you get there. You've got to act quickly or the pizza will be forever gone. Let's say your first action is to *request* the pizza: "Oh hey, I'd like that last slice, actually!" But your friend only rolls their eyes and moves the pizza closer to their mouth. Since your *request* didn't work, you've got to change tactics or you will lose at your objective. You might *reveal* next: "I haven't had anything to eat today." If that doesn't work, you might turn to *guilt*: "So you're just going to hog all of the pizza, huh? You want me to starve?" When that fails, you may *bargain*: "If you give me the pizza, I'll give you the last soda." Like I said, we do this in real life all the time. When one action isn't getting us what we want, and we sense we've hit a dead end, we try something new. This isn't something that we'll explicitly put into the script necessarily. We want to leave interpretation open for actors and directors, but like with action, if we don't think about it, it might not be there later.

In the first chapter, we brainstormed physical actions, and in the action chapter we brainstormed non-physical actions. But since we're about to dive in and get very tactical, let's think up some more actions, both physical and non-physical, so we have plenty ready to go when it's time to try this new tool out.

PHYSICAL ACTIONS: BRAINSTORMING

We'll start with **physical actions**. If you have any from your previous list that you absolutely love, write them down again! Don't think. Just write. There are no wrong answers!

Examples:

- Hug
- Punch
- Kiss

Get your timer ready. Give yourself at least two minutes. Ready? GO!

NON-PHYSICAL ACTIONS: BRAINSTORMING

These are the actions we do with our brains. In my example above with that last slice of pizza, there were some great examples of **non-physical actions**. Steal as many as you want from above that you love, or grab some off your previous list.

Examples:

- Confuse
- Manipulate
- Beg

Get your timer ready. Give yourself at least two minutes. Ready? GO!

❮ Interval ❯

- Once the timer sounds, stop writing!
- Stand, stretch, move, shake it out.
- Go back through your list and star or underline your favorites. If you're in a group, have volunteers share their favorites.
- Afterwards, grab a thesaurus and see if there are any variations on the words on your list that you'd like to add.

FIND THE TACTICS

Think back to your favorite stories. Those TV shows, movies, plays, or books you return to again and again, and maybe also know by heart. Can you think of scenes in which a character quickly changes their action in order to get what they want? Or, can you think of characters that often change tactics as they try to reach their objective?

- List examples
    - How would you describe their changing **actions**?
    - What prompts their shift to new **tactics**?
- Challenge yourself with a timer, or with a minimum number of examples.

This is another area to watch as you consume stories!

TACTICS SCENE

Now that we have our lists, let's dive back into our backstage world of *Romeo and Juliet*. I've got to say, I'm pulling for this production but I'm also pretty nervous for them.

(ASSISTANT STAGE MANAGER sits on the set with NURSE.)

ASSISTANT STAGE MANAGER: Thank you for meeting me before rehearsal.

NURSE: No problemo.

ASSISTANT STAGE MANAGER: Do you know why I asked you here?

NURSE: I think I have a pretty good idea.

ASSISTANT STAGE MANAGER: Okay, phew. I was worried this was going to be awkward.

NURSE: I'm already in a committed relationship. So . . .

ASSISTANT STAGE MANAGER: Oh, uh, I'm not asking you out.

NURSE: Oh. Really?

ASSISTANT STAGE MANAGER: Yeah, no, definitely not.

NURSE: Oh. Well then.

ASSISTANT STAGE MANAGER: I didn't mean . . . You are a very nice person.

NURSE: I know that.

ASSISTANT STAGE MANAGER: And plenty attractive.

NURSE: Obviously.

ASSISTANT STAGE MANAGER: This is a strictly professional situation. This meeting. I asked you to meet up with me now because you're behind. On memorization.

NURSE: Oh.

ASSISTANT STAGE MANAGER: The Stage Manager wanted me to chat with you about it. Come up with a plan.

NURSE: Nah. I'm good.

ASSISTANT STAGE MANAGER: You're supposed to be off book at this point in the rehearsal process.

NURSE: I'm very close to being off book.

ASSISTANT STAGE MANAGER: You called for every single one of your lines yesterday.

NURSE: I don't think it was every single line—

ASSISTANT STAGE MANAGER: It was! I marked them in my script, see?

(ASSISTANT STAGE MANAGER shows NURSE their script.)

NURSE: Well, that's not how I remember it.

ASSISTANT STAGE MANAGER: But I marked it, see the ticks? I mark it so then neither of us have to remember, we have proof.

NURSE: Sure sure, "proof."

ASSISTANT STAGE MANAGER: It IS proof! And not air-quotes proof, actual proof! All of your lines are marked! You have nothing memorized!

NURSE: According to you.

ASSISTANT STAGE MANAGER: And my script where I keep evidence of what happened yesterday in rehearsal!

(NURSE pulls out her script.)

NURSE: Okay, but look at my script. Zero tick marks.

ASSISTANT STAGE MANAGER: Why would there be tick marks in your script? Your script stayed in your bag yesterday because it was our first stumble-through!

NURSE: I'm just saying, if tick marks are proof, the absence of tick marks are also proof.

ASSISTANT STAGE MANAGER: That makes no sense! You make absolutely no . . . Okay. Okay. Yes, there are no tick marks in your script. That is true.

NURSE: It is a FACT.

ASSISTANT STAGE MANAGER: Right. A fact. So your position is that you're basically off book?

NURSE: Basically. Yeah.

ASSISTANT STAGE MANAGER: Then let's run lines. Put your script down.

NURSE: I will if you will.

ASSISTANT STAGE MANAGER: I don't know your cues by heart!

NURSE: The Stage Manager wants everyone to be off book. Uh-oh, you might be in trouble.

ASSISTANT STAGE MANAGER: I'm not in trouble! I'm not acting in the play!

NURSE: I don't know if that matters.

ASSISTANT STAGE MANAGER: Can I just help you? Can I help you to learn your lines? Maybe we could get coffee and—

NURSE: And now you're back to trying to spend more one-on-one time with me! I told you, I am in a committed relationship!

ASSISTANT STAGE MANAGER: FOR THE LAST TIME, I DON'T WANT TO DATE YOU!

NURSE: You can't date me, I am taken.

ASSISTANT STAGE MANAGER: Learn your lines. Can you please just learn your lines?

NURSE: I mostly know them. I told you.

ASSISTANT STAGE MANAGER: We need more than mostly. We need 100 percent.

NURSE: 100 percent? That is asking a LOT.

ASSISTANT STAGE MANAGER: It is literally the bare minimum!!

NURSE: I think if I'm going to learn every single line, I'm going to need some help. Do you think you'd help me run lines?

ASSISTANT STAGE MANAGER: . . . Yeah . . . Yeah, I could do that.

NURSE: Great! Thank you!

(NURSE exits. End of scene.)

➤ Scene Study ❮

- Go back through the scene:
  - Write a verb next to each line to describe the character's **action** (it's fine if words repeat).
  - Are there any lines that start with one **tactic** and end with a different one?
  - Which character has more **tactical** shifts?

Writing Cue ➤➤

Now it's your turn. Pick at least five different active words from your new lists. One of the two characters in this scene will go through all of those actions as their tactics need to change in order to achieve their objective. To be very clear, your scene will:

- Have two characters.
- Both characters will have **objectives**.
- Both will use **actions** in order to reach their **objectives**.
- One will use all FIVE **active** words you selected, changing **tactics** whenever they feel their current **action** isn't getting them closer to their **objective**.

Get your timer ready. Give yourself at least ten to fifteen minutes. Ready? GO!

❮ Interval ❯

- Once the timer sounds, stop writing!
- Stand, stretch, move, shake it out.
- How did that feel?
    - Was anything surprising?
    - Was anything harder than you expected? Easier than expected?
- Read your own scene out loud, playing both characters. Or, if you're in a group, have volunteers share their work.
    - Describe each **action**.
    - Identify each **tactical** shift.
    - Why did the character **shift** their tactics?

ENCORE: ANTI-TACTICS SCENE

I said before that in real life we can sense when an action is failing, so we change tactics. But you know what else is also very true? Sometimes we *don't* sense it. Or sometimes we do sense it, but we don't care. We can be obstinate and stubborn creatures who double down when the logical move would be to try something new. Let's see what it looks like when a character refuses to adapt.

(COSTUME DESIGNER and BENVOLIO are in the costume shop. BENVOLIO is trying on his costume.)

COSTUME DESIGNER: How does that fit, nothing too tight?

BENVOLIO: It fits okay, I guess. I just wish there were more pockets.

COSTUME DESIGNER: What are you talking about, there are plenty of pockets!

BENVOLIO: Not enough, though. I want so many more pockets! It's not fair.

COSTUME DESIGNER: Why would you need more pockets? You have two in the pants, and two more in the jacket.

BENVOLIO: I want my character to be a magician, and if I don't have enough pockets, I won't be able to have all my tricks. But no one cares! No one is helping me.

COSTUME DESIGNER: This is the first I'm hearing that Benvolio is a magician, I had no idea—

BENVOLIO: Not officially. The Director told me I absolutely can't do magic onstage. It's the worst.

COSTUME DESIGNER: I see.

BENVOLIO: No one understands! No one wants me to be happy.

COSTUME DESIGNER: Right. Well, I have a lot of other costume fittings to get to—

BENVOLIO: Magic is the best and if no one gives me a chance to practice my tricks I'm never going to get better at it.

COSTUME DESIGNER: But this is a play? Not a magic show?

BENVOLIO: But there will be an audience and everything! Do you know how many times I've tried to get an audience for my magic tricks?

COSTUME DESIGNER: I'm guessing a lot.

BENVOLIO: So much! But no one will come. That's why I need more pockets. But you probably won't give them to me because nothing can ever go my way.

COSTUME DESIGNER: I really don't care. If you can get the Director to approve more pockets, I can figure something out for you.

BENVOLIO: You're just saying that! You don't care if anyone ever sees my magic.

COSTUME DESIGNER: I'm trying to help you out the best I can.

BENVOLIO: No you're not. No one ever helps me! No one ever will!

(BENVOLIO storms out of the costume shop.)

COSTUME DESIGNER: Hey! HEY! I need that costume! HEY!

(End of scene.)

› Scene Study ‹

- Which of the two characters isn't changing their **tactics**?
- What single **action** would you say the character is using?
- Can you identify the **tactics** that the other character in the scene uses?

Writing Cue ››

And now it's your turn! Here are the parameters for your scene:

- Two characters.
- Both with **objectives.**
- Both use **actions** in order to achieve their **objectives.**

- One of the two characters will refuse to be **tactical**, using only a single **action** throughout the scene.
- The other character can change **tactics**, or if you'd like a real challenge, have them both stick with only one.
- As before, if you'd like to steal the setup from the above scene, please do!

Get your timer ready. Give yourself at least ten to fifteen minutes. Ready? GO!

❮ Interval ❯

- Once the timer sounds, stop writing!
- Stand, stretch, move, shake it out.
- How did that feel?
    - Was anything surprising?
    - Was anything harder than you expected? Easier than expected?
- Read your own scene out loud, playing both characters. Or, if you're in a group, have volunteers share their scenes.
    - Which of the two characters doesn't change their **tactics**?
    - How does it influence the scene?
    - How does it make you feel about the character that isn't changing?
    - Did the character who didn't change obtain their **objective**?

ENCORE: TACTICS BONANZA

Ready to go absolutely wild with **tactics**?

- Get slips of paper ready!
    - Use as few as ten, or go big and challenge yourself! Try for twenty! Or fifty? Sky's the limit.
- Write an **action** on each slip.
- Fold the slips.
- Add each folded slip of paper into a bucket, bowl, or hat.
- Shake them up!
- If you are in a group, mix everyone's slips of paper up together!

Before anyone opens a slip, in this scene, you will need:

- Two characters.
- Both of whom have **objectives**.
- Both of whom use **actions** in order to work toward their **objectives**.
- Slips of **actions** within reach (at least ten per person, more is always okay!)
- **Still don't open them!**

Get a timer ready. Give yourself two minutes. Ready?

- Open the first slip. AND GO!
- Once the two minute timer goes off, open another slip. One of the characters in your scene will now change their **tactics** and use this new **action**.

- Reset your timer. Give yourself another two minutes. GO!
- Repeat this process until everyone has run through their slips. Remember, these do NOT need to make sense. We're working on our writing muscles, not trying to make any kind of logical sense.
- Feel free to increase or decrease the slips; do what works for you or your group!

❮ Interval ❯

- Once the final timer sounds, and you're out of slips, stop writing!
- Stand, stretch, move, shake it out.
- How did that feel?
    - Was anything surprising?
    - Was anything harder than you expected? Easier than expected?
- Read your own scene out loud, playing both characters. Or, if you're in a group, ask for volunteers to share.
    - What were the different **actions**?
    - How did the ever-changing **tactics** change the scene?

SPOTLIGHT ON TACTICS

With **conflict** and **obstacles** we talked about torturing our characters, about how in order to show how much they **want** their **objective** and how much is at **stake** for them, most characters will suffer. **Tactics** are how they can fight back. Tactics are a character's bag of tricks. Every character will have a different bag, just like every person has a different bag. Some bags will be large and varied, some will only have a few choices within.

Sarah Boyd, from my play *Burst,* has a U-Haul truck full of tactics. She runs her company like she's going to war, and her second-in-command, Jennifer Weaver, doesn't agree with that strategy. They are in conflict for the entire full-length, single-scene play, and neither make it easy for the other. To add on the conflict, a reporter comes for a fluff interview, which turns out to be an unflinching exposé of Sarah Boyd and her company. Sarah has a menagerie of tactics at hand and deploys them as deftly as a cat while trying to handle the disaster the evening is quickly dissolving into. She was a fun and challenging character to play with, and we learn a lot about her through her U-Haul truck of tricks, much like we learn about all characters through their actions and tactics.

We equip our characters as they head out to face their battles. Some will be ill-equipped. Some will not be successful. Some will be triumphant. We are in charge of those circumstances, and what our characters bring as they head into battle. What will you give your characters?

. . . Intermission . . .

In Act One, we learned how to **unleash** our inner writer and experimented with essential tools of dramatic writing: **objective**, **action**, **stakes**, **conflict**, **obstacles**, and **tactics**. Continue to use these tools as you write and rewrite.

Act Two will show you how to build a play from start to finish. We will have many exercises before we actually get to writing dialogue in scenes, but never fear! Doing prewriting work will help clarify the project, and give you a solid plan for those inevitable days when you feel a little lost in the trees. The goal of prewriting is to give you direction and inspiration, so that when you pick up those writing tools, you won't have to worry about thinking. If inspiration strikes, and you feel ready to break that blank page, please ride that momentum as long as it takes you. You can always circle back to Act Two to find inspiration again, or to reconsider structure. As in Act One, I will ask you to do some silly things in the following pages. Try to remember the joy and the "play" that is essential to writing plays! You will need it both when the writing flows freely and when it starts to get tricky. Finally, whenever you find yourself in doubt: don't think, just write!

Act Two

BUILDING A PLAY

SPRINGBOARD

EACH SCRIPT STARTS with an infinite number of possibilities, and anytime you narrow it down, your job as a writer gets easier. Finding a **springboard**, or nugget of inspiration, is where I always start. Every step toward what your play *is* builds a pile of what it *isn't*. These are parameters, limits, and they are a gift. They act like a spotlight, giving you a clear idea of what to focus on, just as a spotlight onstage tells the audience where to focus. If I sit down to write a play and I don't know what I want it to be about, I will just stare at a blank page forever. Discovering what parameters help you and your process will not only help you finish a first draft of a play, but also hone your craft as a writer, so that each time you set out to begin a new project, those muscles get stronger and your inner writer is more ready to let loose. It's like deciding on an established trail through the woods, instead of aimlessly wandering. I'll admit, both can be fun, but the trail is much more likely to get you to the spot with the glorious view.

In this chapter we will find a springboard for your new play—a question, topic, story, or character you want to explore. This may change or evolve, but if we don't have that concrete nugget at the start, we run the risk of getting lost in the trees.

WHAT DO I HAVE TO SAY RIGHT NOW?

Humans are all delightfully different; we all have different knowledge and experiences that make us look at the world in our own specific way. When you write, there's no one else that could write exactly like you. And and and, *you* couldn't write a play today the same way you could in ten years. *You* are specific AND *now* is specific. And that's a superpower. Your exact experiences, your exact obsessions, fears, desires, and ways of thinking, all add up to the one and only you right now. A smart writer takes advantage of that and uses that bedrock of specificity and knowledge to report back to the world. So, what do you know about the world that no one else does? What can you tell us about this day? Month? Year? Decade? What can you tell us about being fourteen? Twenty-three? Sixty-seven? What can you tell us about your school? Your job? What can you tell us about where you live? Or the city you grew up in? Your favorite coffee shop? That amusement park that gives you nightmares? The trick is finding the specific nuggets that can turn into stories. How do we do that? If you guessed it would be through **brainstorming** lists, you are correct!

Writing Cue >>

Time to brainstorm! Let anything fall out onto the page in response to these questions. Know that it is up to YOU what you end up sharing; we should only share the parts of ourselves we want to. But for this, like all of our brainstorming, don't think . . . Just write!

Put at least five minutes on a timer for each list, and as usual, don't stop writing until the timer sounds.

1. What People Do You Know?

Unlike in the character brainstorming from the first chapter, I want you to dig deep and get as specific as possible. Does your sister hate the texture of tomatoes and have a deep, dark fear of spiders? Write that down! Who else do you know? Five minutes. GO!

2. What Places Do You Know?

This could be a town, city, apartment, school, or neighborhood park. This could be a room. A closet. List as many specifics as you can. Five minutes. GO!

3. What Are Your Strong Opinions about the World Today?

Are scented candles the worst? Should all schools switch to year-round? What are your strong opinions? Be they small things that only affect you, like your mom using too much mayo on sandwiches, all the way up to the big things that affect the whole planet. Five minutes. GO!

Additional topics/questions to brainstorm:

- What do you love?
- What are you scared of?
- What lessons have you learned?
- What jokes do you know?
- What subjects do you know everything about?

❮ Interval ❯

- Once the final timer sounds, stop writing!
- Stand, stretch, move, shake it out.
- Go back through your list and star or underline anything that grabs you.
- Dig deeper into any answers you underlined, giving yourself two or so minutes on a timer for more freewriting on each.

- If you're in a group, have volunteers share their favorites.

Do any of the items on these lists grab you? Make you lean in? Gets your brain whirling? Maybe that's the starting line for your next play! Any idea *could* be a play; what makes a good idea is how excited that idea makes the author. Writing can be a slog. I don't know any writers who don't have moments of "why, oh why, am I doing this?" Gripping nuggets of inspiration gives you something to hold on to that you are, at least at one point, excited about.

TANGLING WITH THEMES

What themes are you excited to explore in your work? Plot, which we'll get to in a few chapters, concerns what happens in the story, while theme concerns WHY it happens. The main idea. The message. What the audience talks about as they leave the theater. Identifying themes you're interested in exploring can help you find a story. If the theme you want to explore is revenge, you may tell a story about a character avenging their loved one's death, or a rogue gardener's attempt to annihilate all aphids. If you want to talk about friendship, you might tell a story about best friends struggling to stay connected as their lives pull them in opposite directions, or how an unlikely friendship grows between a lion and a zebra.

FIND THE THEME

Think back on your favorite TV shows, books, movies, and plays. What's the idea at the very core of those stories? A phrase or word that reduces the story to its smallest and most essential form? You may even think up multiple themes that fit one story, and that's okay. Themes are subjective. For example, the theme of *Romeo and Juliet* is true love, but it could also be hatred or family loyalty or duality. Theme is in the eye of the beholder.

- Start a list: your favorite example stories in one column, their themes in another.
- Look over your list, is there a common thread through any of the media you love?
- If you're in a group, have volunteers share examples.

Look out for themes in future media consumption. If you find yourself gravitating to similar themes, maybe it's time you explore that theme in your own work! A theme can't be copyrighted, and so you're free to use the same theme as a book, movie, or play that you love.

THE FERTILE GROUND OF THE PAST

If parameters are a trail through the forest of writing, history can provide a map to guide you on the journey. Historical moments can provide characters, settings, and conflicts for you to choose from, like a beautiful gift with purchase. It's a time-honored writing tradition—after all, looking back and commenting on the past is where storytelling began.

History plays shouldn't feel like reading a history textbook. They should sizzle with drama. After all, as the brilliant playwright E. M. Lewis told me before I set off to write my first history play, "It's not history to your characters." All of the people in history plays don't yet know the ups, downs, and endings of their stories, just like we don't know ours.

You may worry that writing from history doesn't speak to the world today, but looking at the mistakes of the past is often said to be the only way not to repeat those same mistakes. The parallels between then and now are plentiful; you as the writer just have to go out and make those connections. Is there a time or event from the past that you find fascinating? Events that you wished the world knew more about or understood better? Or maybe a person that never got the credit they deserved? The past is a forest of stories, just waiting for a hiker to find the most amazing tree and tell the world about it.

BRAINSTORMING THE PAST

Writing Cue ❯❯

Let's get the juices flowing by brainstorming historical moments. And when I say historical, I mean anything that happened before this minute. These can be included in history books or not! They can be small events or world-changing. Anything and everything that interests you—The Great Emu War of Australia, the moon landing, or the invention of the stapler. If you don't know all of the facts, don't worry, there will be time for research later. Get your laptop or writing utensil ready to go. Put five minutes or more on your timer. You'll be writing down a list of as many historical people and events that you can think of. No wrong answers. GO!

❮ Interval ❯

- Once the final timer sounds, stop writing!
- Stand, stretch, move, shake it out.
- Go back through your list and star or underline anything that grabs you.
- If you're in a group, have volunteers share their favorites.

YOUR BEST FRIEND, THE PUBLIC DOMAIN

The final place I'd encourage you to look for inspiration for your next project is in stories that already exist. You might be thinking, but we can't just rewrite existing work, that's stealing! And you're right. It is stealing. But as long as the work is in the public domain, it is world-approved stealing. The public domain is compiled of works whose copyrights have expired. In the US, the copyright of most published work expires ninety-five years after publication. For example, in 2025, works from 1929 entered the public domain, and anyone is free to take those works and adapt them however they see fit.

Taking classic stories everyone knows, or forgotten works that have faded from public awareness, and breathing new life into them through adaptation is a time-honored tradition. After all, if something has survived nearly a hundred years or longer, there must be something exciting that keeps bringing people back. And, like with history plays, a lot of the work is done for you as far as thinking up what will happen and who it will happen to.

And there is such a huge range in direction you can take your version of an existing work. When I first started writing plays, I adapted a lot of Greek myths. Some of my adaptations are close to the originals, and some are complete departures. Just as when you take inspiration from history, you get to decide how much to change and how much to keep. Want to reimagine *Hamlet* in an '80s mall? Or *Oedipus Rex* at an underwater castle with a cast full of mermaids? The beauty of the public domain is that those works belong to all of us, and we can do with them whatever we choose.

Before you jump off and get going with an existing work, it always makes sense to double-check it is, in fact, in the public domain. Keep in mind that lists of public-domain material change every year, and it's always worth checking if something you're itching to adapt will fall into the public domain in the coming years.

SPOTLIGHT ON SPRINGBOARD

Inspiration is all around us. I've listed only a few places to look, but there are countless more. The trick is to build up your inspiration muscles through writing, and (yes!) writing more. Eventually you will start to learn where the best inspiration comes from for you. Look back over all the lists we wrote this chapter. Consolidate everything you starred or underlined into one single list. Of all of those options, which grabs you the most? Again, there are no wrong answers. There's no such thing as wrong inspiration. I have plays in drawers that will never see the light of day, but each one taught me about writing, and more importantly, about how *I* write.

In the very back of my notebook, where I write all of my exercises, brainstorming, and notes on current and upcoming projects, I keep a list of any springboard ideas that come to me that I don't immediately have time to write. My play *Of Serpents and Sea Spray* was on just such a list for more than six months before I pitched it to an artistic director and got it commissioned.

It's also important to not feel pressured that you need to pick the best option. You can always throw out what doesn't work. You can always start fresh. And all those other options will be there waiting for you when you're ready.

Since you need to start somewhere, it's time to pick your springboard. Have one with more than one star? Or one that is underlined twice? Works for me, let's go!

GENRE

LIKE WE JUST LEARNED in the last chapter, parameters, or rules, make life easier for the writer. Each **genre** comes with a set of rules, or expectations, that you can decide to follow or break. If, for example, there is a wedding (or two) at the end of a Shakespeare play, that's a comedy. A whole lot of death? Tragedy. Genres may feel stifling, but understanding the rules can be a gift; just like with your nugget of inspiration, a genre can show you both what your play *is* and *isn't*. At the end of the day, we're in charge, so we get to decide which rules we follow, which rules we bend, and which rules we break. Genre gives us shapes and lines, like in a coloring book, and all we have left to do is get to coloring.

COMEDY AND DRAMA

When I close my eyes and try to think of the most iconic symbol of theatre, the comedy and drama masks are the first image that pops into my head. And genre can really be as simple as that. Does a story *mostly* make people laugh? Does a story *mostly* make people feel? There are a lot more nitty-gritty details, but that's the basics of genre, and it's from these two massive categories that all genres spring.

There are rules for both, especially comedies, but when I start a new project, one of the first things I want to know is: will this be a comedy or a drama? The first play I ever wrote, I sent to my two best friends to read, and later, after they'd read it, we hopped on a call and they said, "Rachel, it's so funny!" To which I responded: ". . . . . It's not supposed to be." The moment was a bit of a blow, but after we chatted more, I realized my friends were right, and knowing what that play was helped me shape it later in rewrites, and allowed me to find a lot more funny moments.

FIND THE GENRES

Speaking of examples, let's find examples of TV shows, movies, musicals, and plays that fit into either comedy or drama! Giving yourself one minute for each of the genres. How many examples of each can you think of? If you're looking for a challenge, limit yourself to examples from plays and musicals only! Ready? GO!

- Go through your lists. Did you list any title under both **genres**?
    - Respond to why you felt it could be categorized both ways.
- Was one **genre** easier to make a list for than the other?
    - **Genre** you found it more difficult to think up examples of?
    - Consider seeking out works that fit into the **genre** you had a harder time thinking of titles for.
- If you're in a group, have volunteers share the examples they found.

EXPLORING SUBGENRES

Subgenres are specific subcategories of story, each with their own set of characteristics and traits. The benefit of zeroing in on a subgenre is that each comes with even more rules and parameters. They work as an add-on to any genre. For example, you can have a comedic fantasy or a horror drama or a romantic comedy or a science-fiction drama or even a dramedy, which combines both comedy and drama. Like a fun mix and match! As with genres, it is helpful to learn more about these subgenres before you jump in. Learning what the audience expects from each will give you an understanding of where the lines of these particular subgenres rest.

Here's a very incomplete list of subgenres to get your brain percolating on options:

- Melodrama
- Farce
- Satire
- Science Fiction
- Romance
- Horror
- Mystery

But there are a lot more out there, right? Absolutely. Why don't we brainstorm subgenres!

BRAINSTORMING SUBGENRES

What subgenres did I leave off my list? Give yourself at least one minute and write down as many subgenres you can think of. Ready? GO!

- After your timer goes off, go through your list. What **subgenres** are you drawn to?

   - Define the **subgenres** that get you excited. Feel free to look up rules and/or definitions as you explore.
- If you're in a group, have volunteers share their lists.

FIND THE SUBGENRE

What examples can you think of that fall into each subgenre? You can pull from TV shows, plays, movies, or musicals. Like before, if you're looking for a challenge, only list examples meant to live onstage. Give yourself at least one minute for each subgenre, and feel free to add any additional subgenres you may have thought up yourself. Ready? GO!

- Go through your lists. Did you list any title under two different **subgenres**?
- Which **subgenre** was the easiest to find examples of?
- Which was the hardest?
- Consider seeking out works that fit into the **subgenres** you had a harder time thinking up examples of.
- If you're in a group, have volunteers share some examples.

PLAYING WITH SUBGENRE: MELODRAMA SCENE

In order to see how genres can shape a project, let's take a scene from Act One, throw a genre on top of it, and see how that changes things. This scene is from the chapter on **conflict**, the "Direct Conflict Scene." The characters struggle with what they should order for dinner: pizza or Chinese food. What happens if we make the scene a melodrama?

(SET DESIGNER and LIGHTING DESIGNER are onstage. They paint a wall, adding details to make it look like a castle wall.)

SET DESIGNER: That ivy detail, it's absolutely beautiful.

LIGHTING DESIGNER: Thank you, I'm letting the muse be my guide.

SET DESIGNER: Your talent is enviable. You're wasted as a lighting designer.

LIGHTING DESIGNER: Perhaps in another life, I designed sets, like yourself. But I must follow my passion, and even with my talent for painting, my passion lies with illumination.

SET DESIGNER: How will I ever repay you for lending me your talent? Please, you must allow me to do something for you.

LIGHTING DESIGNER: I do find myself rather famished.

SET DESIGNER: You're hungry, dear friend? It would be an honor to feed someone so talented and generous.

LIGHTING DESIGNER: Now you are the one who is being generous! I'll take you up on your offer, and I propose the most perfect of dinner options: Chinese food! The Golden Dragon will bring to us dishes slathered in delectable spices and seasonings over pillow-soft rice or noodles so silky—

SET DESIGNER: Chinese food? Is that what your heart desires?

LIGHTING DESIGNER: But of course! How could a heart desire anything else?

SET DESIGNER: Chinese food is delicious, I will admit, but I answer your suggestion with one of my own: pizza.

LIGHTING DESIGNER: Don't you bore of the repetition? I have seen you consume nothing but pizza for the past four days and four nights!

SET DESIGNER: And you would deny me, your dearest friend, the opportunity to achieve a perfect pizza week?

LIGHTING DESIGNER: You put me in an impossible position! You desire pizza, I desire anything but pizza!

SET DESIGNER: Name for me one other type of food that could even hope to compete with the utter brilliance of pizza!

LIGHTING DESIGNER: I have already made my suggestion, and I would argue that the variety offered on The Golden Dragon's menu far outstrips that of any pizza parlor!

SET DESIGNER: You wound me greatly.

LIGHTING DESIGNER: I do not wish to wound you. I only wish for you to open your mind to other possibilities! There is a particularly wonderful spicey chicken noodle dish—

SET DESIGNER: If it's chicken you must have, Pizza Palace has barbecue chicken pizza options!

LIGHTING DESIGNER: Chicken, barbecue, and pizza is a horrifying combination! Just the thought of eating it is shameful!

SET DESIGNER: Well I would be ashamed to consume anything but pizza! And since it is I who is paying, who is so generously offering to feed you. I hate to say it, but you may not have much choice in the matter.

LIGHTING DESIGNER: No choice? I could always take my paint brush and walk away.

SET DESIGNER: You wouldn't!

LIGHTING DESIGNER: I would.

SET DESIGNER: You would really so easily walk away from this project? You gave me your word that you would assist me!

LIGHTING DESIGNER: My word I did give, but I never declared I would see it to its completion. Have I not painted enough ivy?

SET DESIGNER: But there are four more pillars needing that detail!

LIGHTING DESIGNER: And could you not finish them? You are the set designer, after all!

SET DESIGNER: They would be inferior to those that you've already completed! Don't you see? The play would suffer from your desertion!

LIGHTING DESIGNER: Then save the play, order Chinese!

SET DESIGNER: Must you really be so obstinate? Can't you help me finish the ivy and eat some excellent pizza? I will let you select all of the toppings!

LIGHTING DESIGNER: I'm sorry, but on my honor, I will not eat pizza tonight!

SET DESIGNER: Then buy your own dinner, if you are so set against pizza!

LIGHTING DESIGNER: If only I could! Do you not understand? I am generous with my talents for the sake of the play, yes, but also for the stake of my stomach. You see, I am completely broke until opening night.

SET DESIGNER: It is not on my head that you are out of money. I will order pizza, enough to feed us both. Do your stomach a favor and eat what you are given!

LIGHTING DESIGNER: I am saddened to hear you say that. I must go and see if the Costume Designer needs my assistance. I am as good with a needle and thread as I am with a paintbrush, you know.

SET DESIGNER: But, but, the ivy!

LIGHTING DESIGNER: If you order The Golden Dragon, all the ivy will be finished—on that you have my word.

SET DESIGNER: I will not stand for this coercion! I am funding this meal and pizza it will be! In fact I will not just order enough pizza for myself and for you, but I will include our dear Costume Designer as well. You can eat it, or you can go hungry.

(SET DESIGNER exits to order pizza. LIGHTING DESIGNER shakes their fist.)

LIGHTING DESIGNER: Curse you, pizza! Curse you!

(End of scene.)

➤ Scene Study ❮

The scene above changes a lot adding on the genre of melodrama to it from the original. What did you notice?

- How does **genre** affect the characters?
- How does **genre** affect the language?
- How does **genre** affect the stakes?
- How else does **genre** affect this scene?

Writing Cue ➤➤

And now it's your turn to play with subgenres! Pick a subgenre and one of the scenes you wrote in Act One. You will take the basic elements of that scene—characters, objectives, time, and place—and rewrite it with a new genre in mind.

You will need:

- A **subgenre**. Either one listed above, or one that you brainstormed.
- A scene previously written for one of Act One's exercises.

Get a timer ready. Give yourself twenty minutes. GO!

❮ Interval ❯

- Stop writing once the timer goes off.
- Stand, stretch, move, shake it out.
- How did that feel?
- Read your scene out loud. Or, if you're in a group, ask for volunteers to share.
    - What effect did **subgenre** have on:
        - **Character**?
        - **Objective**?
        - **Action**?
        - **Stakes**?
    - What else changed in the scene?

PLAYING WITH SUBGENRE TAKE TWO: MYSTERY SCENE

Let's try that again! We'll take a scene from Act One and rewrite it with a different subgenre in mind. For this example, we'll use the encore "Counterintuitive Action Scene" and put the subgenre of mystery on it. What will happen?

(Outside the theater, JULIET enters from a theater exit. She pulls out keys. NURSE enters from the same theater exit.)

NURSE: Rehearsal is about to start! Where are you going?

JULIET: Oh, I, uh, I left, um, stuff, something I really need, it's in my car.

NURSE: Can't you get it later? The Director will flip if you're not there!

JULIET: Oh, but I'll be back. I'm just going to my car for, uh, that thing.

NURSE: I heard that you have a bit of stage fright?

JULIET: What? Who would say that? That's, that's flat-out bonkers! And wrong. So wrong.

NURSE: It's okay, you know. It's not a big deal. Lots of people get stage fright.

JULIET: You think?

NURSE: Oh yeah, tons. Pretty sure it's up there with the most common fears.

JULIET: I didn't want as big a role as *Juliet,* you know? I didn't expect— I thought I'd play a nonspeaking part! Like a tree!

NURSE: Relax, we'll get you through this. I'm the expert on combating stage fright!

JULIET: Then you've dealt with it too?

NURSE: Me? No. Never. Not my style.

JULIET: Oh.

NURSE: But I do know a lot of things you should be MORE scared of than just talking in front of strangers.

JULIET: Oh, well I don't think—

NURSE: Like, for example, did you know that a surprising number of people DIE onstage?

JULIET: What?

NURSE: Just boom. Dead! Mostly choking. It's surprisingly hard to eat and drink onstage. But you don't have to eat or drink ANYthing, so you won't have to worry about that!

JULIET: . . . Okay . . .

NURSE: But those are just the natural deaths. You should probably keep an eye out for an *un*natural death. Just to be on the safe side. You would be surprised by how many people have died on our stage.

JULIET: Wait, *un*natural death? People have had an *un*natural death on this stage?

NURSE: Oh yeah. Surprised you didn't know. It's a popular case among the unsolved murder lot.

JULIET: I'm sorry, wait, there was a murder? On this stage? And it's unsolved? I have so many questions.

NURSE: I don't know everything. I just know it was two summers ago, the Assistant Stage Manager.

JULIET: How did it happen?

NURSE: Poison.

JULIET: Wow. Wow, wow, wow.

NURSE: I know! So when you compare being poisoned to just speaking in front of people, the speaking in front of people doesn't sound half bad, now does it?

JULIET: No, that's still pretty terrifying . . . But . . .

NURSE: But?

JULIET: But maybe I should stick it out, my dad was . . . My dad was a detective, so I know a thing or two about unsolved murders.

NURSE: I'm glad to hear you'll stick it out, but word to the wise, I wouldn't stick my nose in this. A lot of people from that production are working on this production, and they might not like you digging. I'd put good money on one of them being the murderer.

JULIET: They should have thought of that before they murdered that poor Assistant Stage Manager. Now come on, we have to get back into rehearsal, everyone will be wondering where we are.

(NURSE and JULIET exit, back into the theater. End of scene.)

Scene Study

In the example above you can see me lean into things we see again and again in the subgenre of mystery. A detective is in a new place and they either discover a crime or suspects surround them, and they must complete something that they don't want to in order to solve the case. That's one of the gifts of subgenres. They come with a lot of common ground, which you get to use or ignore.

- What effect did **subgenre** have on:
  - **Character**?
  - **Objective**?
  - **Action**?
  - **Stakes**?
- Any other changes to the scene?

Writing Cue ❯❯

Another chance to play with subgenres! We'll repeat the subgenre exercise with a new subgenre, as well as one of the scenes that you wrote in Act One. Rewrite that scene with the subgenre in mind. To be clear, you will need:

- A **subgenre** from the list above, or one you brainstormed.
- A scene previously written from one of Act One's exercises.

Get a timer ready. Give yourself twenty minutes. GO!

❮ Interval ❯

- Stop writing once the timer goes off.
- Stand, stretch, move, shake it out.
- How did that feel?
- Read your scene out loud, or if you're in a group, have volunteers share.
    - What effect did **subgenre** have on:
        - **Character**?
        - **Objective**?
        - **Action**?
        - **Stakes**?
    - Any other changes to the scene?

SPOTLIGHT ON GENRE

When I was wrapping up the first draft of my sci-fi comedy play *Cheerleaders VS. Aliens*, I struggled with what would happen with my cheerleaders after they'd kicked alien butt and sent those aliens packing. It was leaning into genre that gave me my answer. Comedies end with weddings. Now these characters were high school students, so literal weddings wouldn't work, but how could I interpret the idea of "weddings" for modern-day high-school students? In the play, the cheerleaders and rescued football players throw a giant dance party, two of my characters head off into the night to get hot chocolate hand in hand, and my character who started the play with no friends finds herself surrounded by people that suddenly appreciate her. It was a fun way to finish the play, and leaning into the genre gave me that ending. Genre has a lot to offer you too.

Remember, selecting a genre and/or subgenre for your new play gives you rules to work with or against. It's a trick that took me years of writing to figure out. And the best news? If you pick a genre for your first draft and decide it isn't working, change it in draft two! Nothing is permanent, and you are (always) the boss.

TIME AND PLACE

MY NEXT STEP IN PREGAMING MY PLAY is to work out the **time** and **place**. Where will this play happen? When will this play take place? Both have a huge impact on your story. An argument at two in the afternoon will be different from an argument at two in the morning. Additionally, an argument in an empty warehouse will always be different than an argument in the nursery with a baby that's just gone down for a nap. Time and place impacts your characters and story tremendously, and gives you more parameters to work within.

So where would be the best place to tell this story? When is the best time? Yet again, there is no correct answer. It's something for you to decide and then feel out. Luckily, it's another aspect that can be changed later in rewrites. Gotta love those rewrites.

BRAINSTORMING PLACES

Writing Cue ❯❯

I want you to have your springboard in your mind, and I want you to also think about the genre and subgenre you're going for. With that information, give yourself two minutes (or up to five minutes if you want a challenge) and write down as many different locations that you can think of. These don't have to make any sense. Like I've said before, we have a lot of extra junk banging around in our brains and sometimes it helps just to get some of the nonsense out on paper. Alternatively, if you don't want to use a timer, give yourself a number, maybe twenty, or go really big with fifty or one hundred. Sit down and write locations until you've listed out that many options. These can be as specific as you want. For example, if you name a small town, you may want to list all the places within that small town that you could have a scene. Ready with your timer or number? GO!

❮ Interval ❯

- Stand, stretch, move, shake it out.
- Look over your lists:
    - Star or underline your favorite places.
- For each location you underlined, think about or write out the benefits and the complications.
- If you're in a group, have volunteers share their favorite places they listed.

WHAT ABOUT TIME?

Time is twofold. It's helpful to know when we are history—as in the year 1923, or modern day, or the year 2451—but it's also good to know in a more detailed way—as in a Monday at 4:50 p.m., or Christmas morning. I don't think that you need to know every detail of time before you jump into writing; however, it is incredibly helpful to think about when you are, as the play changes if it's set in the year 1950 compared to 2050.

What if you want to move backward in time as your play moves forward? Or jump around back and forth? Or maybe each scene will jump forward one hundred years into the future? All of this is possible. It's important to go back to your springboard and think about when is the best time to tell this story? When will it have the most impact? As long as you keep in mind what is essential to the story you are trying to tell, you can play with time all day long. After all, we're here to "play" and that involves a lot of imagination.

BRAINSTORMING TIMES

Writing Cue ❯❯

So let's get some options for when your play takes place. Think about your springboard, genre, and subgenre, as well as where you're planning to set the story. From that information, when will it have the most impact for your play to take place? In your brainstorming, start with the larger units of time—focusing more on centuries, decades, or specific years—and then move to the more detailed units of time—as in season, day, and time of day.

Okay! Get a timer ready for two minutes, and keep in mind all those ideas we have bopping around and the work you've already done for this play. Remember to let terrible ideas out along with great ones. Once you're in a comfortable spot with your writing utensil of choice, hit start on that timer. That's right, GO!

❮ Interval ❯

- Stand, stretch, move, shake it out.
- Look over your lists:
    - Star or underline your favorite **times**.

- For each time you underlined, think about or write out the benefits and the complications of each.
    - Also think about how your favorite **times** will impact your favorite **places** you listed earlier in the chapter.
- If you're in a group, have volunteers share their favorite **times** from their list.

TIME AND PLACE SCENE

Now that we've brainstormed and thought a bit about how time and place can change a scene, let's see it in action! We'll take the "Showing Character Through Action Scene" from Act One and change the time and place and see what that does to the characters.

(The library. Seven in the morning. PARIS paces. HEAD OF PUBLICITY enters. Both the HEAD OF PUBLICITY and PARIS whisper.)

HEAD OF PUBLICITY: I was able to talk to the Director.

PARIS: And?

HEAD OF PUBLICITY: And, they're pretty upset. It's early in the morning, and they were sleeping, and they really would have preferred me to wait until a more reasonable time to just show up at their house and knock on their door asking questions—

PARIS: That is not what I meant—

HEAD OF PUBLICITY: Or just wait until rehearsal later today—

PARIS: What about *me*, did you ask—

HEAD OF PUBLICITY: It was for sure the wrong call to go over and wake the Director up. No one wants to be awake this early. Why are we awake this early?

PARIS: Obviously because this is an emergency situation! Are we switching roles?

HEAD OF PUBLICITY: No. The cast will stay as is. No role switching.

PARIS: Unbelievable. UNbeLIEVABLE! I can't believe it. Can you believe it?

HEAD OF PUBLICITY: I mean . . .

PARIS: *(Not whispering:)* WHAT?!

HEAD OF PUBLICITY: Dude, this is a library, you have to keep it down!

PARIS: *(Back to whispering:)* Sorry, I'm just. It's all so unbelievable. It's like the Director wants this production to fail. Did you mention that I would be significantly better in the role? Maybe you should go back, maybe—

HEAD OF PUBLICITY: I almost got fired. I'm not going back. Especially not before nine. It's not polite.

PARIS: *(Yelling:)* I DON'T CARE ABOUT BEING POLITE! I CARE THAT I GET CAST AS ROMEO!

HEAD OF PUBLICITY: Wow, I can't— You can't just yell in a public library at seven in the morning! I don't care how upset you are about casting. Not cool, not cool at all.

(HEAD OF PUBLICITY exits.)

PARIS: But this is an emergency! We have to fix this!!

(PARIS exits, following the HEAD OF PUBLICITY. End of scene.)

❯ Scene Study ❮

- How does the different **time** change the scene?
- How does the different **place** change the scene?

Writing Cue ❯❯

Your turn to play with time and place! Take one of your scenes from Act One, and put it in a different time and place. Take advantage of the lists we brainstormed earlier in this chapter for your new location and time. (Hint, this is more fun if you make a big shift in the time and place!) You will need:

- A specific **place**, different from where your scene was originally set.
- A specific **time**, different from when your scene was originally set.
- A scene previously written for one of Act One's exercises.

Get a timer ready. Give yourself fifteen minutes. GO!

❮ Interval ❯

- Stop writing once the timer goes off.
- Stand, stretch, move, shake it out.
- How did that feel?
- Read your scene out loud. Or, if you're working in a group, have volunteers share.

- How does the different **time** affect the scene?
- How does the different **place** affect the scene?

SPOTLIGHT ON TIME AND PLACE

We're in the game of imagination, or *play*ing. I don't know about you, but I can imagine quite a lot. A lot more than I could ever hope to sit down and actually write in a lifetime. Getting ahold of all the details that will eventually become your play before you start to write gives you the gift of parameters to focus your imagination.

In my play *The Book Women,* the time and place are super specific: it takes place over one day in the late summer of 1939 in Breathitt County, Kentucky. Setting the play so specifically gave me so many parameters to play within, as well as research avenues to explore. I listened to people talk from that place and time to learn how my characters should talk. Kentucky happens to have an amazing oral library that I was able to take advantage of. The play would have been a different play set in another time, or another place. Setting it when I did allowed me to find details that make it feel three-dimensional and complex.

Time and place also happens to be one of the elements I will play with in rewrites the most. Does something feel too easy for one of my characters? Let's make this scene happen at midnight then, or take my character away from their comfort zone and have the scene take place squarely on their nemesis's turf. I encourage you to play with time and place with your writing exercises moving forward, and also in the first draft of your play. You get more of those wonderful parameters, along with details and specificity.

CHARACTERS

AFTER I HAVE my **springboard**, an idea of **genre**, and a **time** and **place**, I start to explore **characters**. Who should tell this story? Characters are your vehicle. Not only do we hear the story through characters' dialogue, but through characters we also learn about the world of the play, the other characters in the play, and everyone's relationships. A character's journey will become the structure of your play. And finally, since the audience craves the stage to mirror real life, it is through the characters that they experience the story being told. We want to see people strive and try and fail and succeed, and we want to learn what their journey says about our own.

WHERE DO CHARACTERS COME FROM?

It's a tall order. Making up some humans out of thin air! Luckily our imaginations are up to the task. We'll go through a series of questions and thinking points in this section, giving you the ability to flesh your characters out in some detail. Feel free to repeat these steps for as many characters as you plan to have in your play.

Before I get into the information gathering, I want to state that while I refer to all characters in this section as humans, not all characters are human. Some characters are horses, or trees, or the Pacific Ocean. For our purposes I will continue to only mention humanoid characters, but feel free to replace that word with whatever character you're making.

HOW MANY CHARACTERS FIT IN THIS PLAY?

How do you decide how many characters you need for your play? I start with my main character, and work out from there. Will anyone be helping them? As in best friend/partner/sidekick? Will anyone be standing in their way? As in antagonist/nemesis/enemy? Will anyone be advising them? As in teacher/mentor? Will there be romance? As in a love interest or, making things very interesting, two love interests? Sounds like it's time to do some writing . . .

Writing Cue ➤➤

A timer is not essential for this exercise, but if you absolutely must live by that structure, give yourself a full twenty minutes. This is what I want you to think about:

- Going back to your **springboard**, WHO is essential to tell this story?
- Thinking about the **genre** and **subgenre** you landed on, who do you normally find in those stories? Are you going to work within the mold, or break the rules?
- Think about **setting**. What **characters** do we automatically associate with that **setting**? Where do you want to embrace this association and where do you want to challenge it?
    - For example, a backstage play about *Romeo and Juliet* will have all the characters of the play, plus designers, plus a director, and other theater support personnel as potential characters for the play.

- Think about **objectives** and **obstacles**:
    - Does one of the characters hold the key to an **objective**?
    - Does one of the characters stand in the way as an **obstacle**?

❮ Interval ❯

- Stop writing once the timer goes off.
- Stand, stretch, move, shake it out.
- How did that feel?
- Look over your list of potential characters:
    - Which feel essential to the story?
        - Underline or star these!
    - Are there any that don't feel essential?
    - If you're in a group, have volunteers share a few of their characters.

Keep this rough sketch handy, we'll be adding to it as we get through more character details and ultimately bring these characters somewhat to life!

CHARACTER YOU CAN'T FORGET

We've all seen and read characters we can't forget. Sometimes we love them, sometimes we hate them, but either way they live in our heads, sometimes for entire decades. These characters have the audience rooting for them to fail or to succeed. Either way there is no denying that these characters have gotten under our skins. So how can we create characters like this? There are no hard and fast rules to live by . . . As playwrights we don't always get a say in which characters land and click with our audiences. But there are a few guidelines that can help:

Flaws over Flawless

No real person is perfect, and putting too many outstanding characteristics onto one character can make them feel fake. A character that has to grow or change in order to achieve their objective is incredibly relatable. Characters that are too perfect have nothing to learn.

Allow for Contradictions

Real human beings are messy and contradictory. Remember **counterintuitive actions** from Act One? What are situations you can expose your characters to where they feel one way but act in the opposite way?

Someone We Want to Root For over Likability

We can often fall into a trap trying to make our characters "likable," especially female characters. But characters aren't always meant to be liked. After all, if we think of King Richard III, most of the audience won't like him, but they often can't help but root for him because he is both complex and engaging.

Let Your Characters Lead

My final bit of advice for creating complex, dynamic characters is to let them guide you. Do all the pregame work of brainstorming and making choices, but in the moment, when you're writing your play, if a character decides they're going to throw out your plan and go off and do something unexpected, let them. If it surprises and engages you, chances are very good that it will surprise and engage an audience as well.

BEWARE THE PASSIVE PROTAGONIST

We focus so much on our protagonists that sometimes we can develop a bit of a blind spot for their action, or lack of action, and they become passive right under our nose. Meanwhile, their best friend or mortal enemy may have no trouble going after what they want in a highly explosive way. This can be frustrating as you want your protagonist to be the most active and exciting of everyone in your cast. They're kinda the reason for the season, after all. But I think we end up thinking so much about our protagonists that sometimes there's no room for instincts to just wing things and allow them to go off on unplanned adventures.

Never fear! There is a way to combat this focus and the passivity that comes with it . . . Let go of the steering wheel. You've done all this background work; you've thought out every beat of the play. But when you sit down to write, try to let all of that go and let your main character lead you. Of all your characters, give the most credence to your main character and go where they want to go. That's your inner writer working cooperatively with that character, and that's where some serious magic can happen in your pages.

SPOTLIGHT ON CHARACTERS

Characters are the most human part of your script, even if none of your characters are human. And, since they deliver your words, they also leave the biggest impression on your audience. The slightly infuriating part of characters is that after we work so hard to create complex and dynamic characters, they end up getting ideas of their own. Sometimes they go off on unnecessary tangents, but most of the time, any meandering led by your characters is worth it. It's a skill to let go and let your characters lead the way.

In my ensemble murder mystery *Blood and Sequins,* I spent a lot of time figuring out the background and motivations of everyone, but I absolutely gave the most attention to the murderer and their number-one enemy. At the first reading of the play, I was shocked that one of the less central characters, a golden retriever of a young man, completely steals the show. He had laughs after each of his lines. The readers were crushed when he met his end. Why did this character have so much natural jam? Because my brain was busy with other characters and he just got to be. All the work I've had you do on letting go is for this. The majority of my most funny, exciting, and intriguing characters are the ones who are free to walk their own path. Yes, all the prework is needed, but it's equally important not to think when writing.

Repeat after me: don't think! Just write!

STRUCTURE AND PLOT

WE'VE GOT OUR **springboard**, we've settled on **genre** and **subgenre**, we know when and where our play will happen, and we have ideas about who will be in it . . . What's next? **Structure** and **plot**!

Much like a building, a play cannot stand without structure. Structure gives a play its shape, the beams and support that you will eventually fill in to tell the story you want to share with the world. Planning my structure before I dive into a new script is an essential step for me and my writing. But what exactly is structure? And how does structure relate to plot? Because they are, in fact, two different things. We'll start out by getting you comfortable with understanding both terms, and then dive into you drafting the shell of your play.

BASIC STRUCTURE

Structure is tied closely to **characters** and their **objectives**. "Objectives again?," you may be wondering, to which I tell you that if you're considering playwriting, you're gearing up to eat, sleep, and dream objectives.

Plays reflect our world. We crave to watch other humans experience life. It's why we started to gather around fires and tell stories to begin with. It's a tool for learning, building community, and catharsis. We want to watch two people fall in love, so we can have a slice of that experience from our seat in the audience, just like we want to watch them laugh with friends, save the village, and even plot murder. The key ingredient to all of that is: people. We want people, and we want to watch them do people things. People wrestling with emotions. People learning lessons. Structure, at its most basic, is the journey of the people in your story. It works like this:

- Character wants X (beginning)
- Character works to get X (middle)
- Character either gets or doesn't get X (end)

Structure can be as simple as that. And this very basic concept happens again and again over the course of a play as your characters move through the story. The protagonist has an objective, but not just one! As established in Act One, throughout a play, your protagonist will have a macro-objective, which is the main, big objective that they're working toward the entire time, as well as many micro-objectives that they succeed or fail at over the course of the story, which build toward that macro-objective. By the end of the play, because of these battles both big and small, which have moved them toward their macro-objective, your protagonist will either be forever changed, or their world will be. Structure is the character's journey tracked through objectives either reached or failed.

LOOKING AT CLASSIC STRUCTURE

So now that we know the essential, most basic form structure can take, let's take a look at how this classically presents itself. Structure is another tool like genre. Once you've mastered structure, you can defy or embrace structure's expectations. These are rules you learn so you can understand when and how to break them.

Classic structure will have these moments, in this order:

1. Inciting Incident

Often about 10 percent into a play. We've been introduced to the world; we've met the protagonist. Then something flips this world, or protagonist, upside down. This flipping sets the protagonist up for what they want, their macro-objective. Maybe their family gets kidnapped and they want them back, or a dance at school has been announced and they want to ask the most popular kid, or a droid shows up with a hologram from a princess asking for help.

2. Building or Rising Action

This is the bulk of the play. The main character is trying to get their macro-objective, taking care of those smaller micro-objectives that keep popping up along their way. They lose some, they win some, but as the play continues, the objectives become more demanding, and the stakes get raised.

3. Climax

This is the moment! The big moment! This is when the protagonists definitely fails or succeeds to achieve their macro-objective. This is what the entire play has been working toward.

4. Resolution

What happens now? This is the very end of your play. It's also known as "falling action." The macro-objective has been reached or hasn't, and now we get a glimpse at what that means both to our protagonist and the world that they live in.

ENCORE: FIND THE RULE-BREAKING STRUCTURE

Most things embrace classic structure. But what breaks those rules? My favorite example is Samuel Beckett's *Waiting for Godot,* where two characters arrive at a tree in order to meet a third character, Godot, but he never shows, so the whole play is just them *waiting.* What's massively impressive about the script is how active the characters are given this very inactive setup. But there are many other examples!

Have a timer ready with two minutes on it. I want you to list as many examples of movies, plays, musicals, and books that do something different. Ready? GO!

- Pick at least four or five examples that you wrote down, though feel free to do more.
- For each example, ask:
    - How do they break the rules?
    - As an audience, how did the play's bucking of **structure**'s rules affect you?
    - If you had to guess, why do you think the creators decided to play with **structure**?

WELL THEN, WHAT IS PLOT?

Structure is all about **character**; what they *want,* what they *learn,* how they *grow.* **Plot,** on the other hand, is all the stuff that happens along the way. Both structure and plot are concerned with getting your play from the beginning to the end; they are intertwined. Plots, though, are like dominos all lined up on a floor. One plot point feeds into or causes the next point, leading all the way to the climax. For example:

- Juliet is hungry and wants a Big Mac from McDonald's.
- Because she wants a Big Mac, she gets into her car to drive to McDonald's.
- Because she's driving to McDonald's, she starts her car.
- Because she's started her car, she sees that her car has an empty gas tank.
- Because she has no gas, she checks her wallet to find her last $10.
- Because she can't afford both gas and McDonald's, Juliet starts to walk to McDonald's.
- Because she has to walk, Juliet gets even more hungry.
- Because she's even more hungry, she decides to run.
- Because she's running, she doesn't see a crack in the sidewalk.
- Because she doesn't see the crack in the sidewalk, she trips.
- Because she trips, she falls and skins her knee.
- Because she has a skinned knee, she wonders if the Big Mac is worth it.
- Because she wonders if the Big Mac is worth it, she realizes she's hungrier than ever.
- Because she's hungrier than ever, she gets up and limps along toward McDonald's.
- Because she's limping, it takes her much longer to walk.
- Because it takes her so long to walk, the sun goes down.
- Because the sun goes down, it becomes much darker out.
- Because it is much darker out, she gets lost.
- Because she is lost, and hurt, and hungry, she sits down on the curb and starts to cry.

- Because she is sitting down on the curb, she notices a slip of paper blowing down the street.
- Because she notices the slip of paper, she catches it as it flies by.
- Because she catches the slip of paper, she looks at it.
- Because she looks at the slip of paper, she realizes it is an unused scratch-off ticket.
- Because it's an unused scratch-off ticket, she takes out a coin and scratches it off.
- Because she scratches the ticket, it reveals three jackpot symbols in a row.
- Because she's scratched off three jackpot symbols, she stands and starts to walk again.
- Because she starts to walk again, she comes to a corner store that sells scratch-off tickets.
- Because she walks by the corner store, she enters the corner store and hands the winning ticket to the person behind the counter.
- Because she handed the ticket to the person behind the counter, they scan it, and hand over her winnings of $100,000.
- Because she's won $100,000, Juliet calls a cab to get to McDonald's.
- Because she's taken a cab to McDonald's, she arrives at McDonald's.
- Because she's at McDonald's, and because she's just won $100,000, Juliet buys everyone there two Big Macs.
- Because she now has two Big Macs, she eats both burgers.
- Because she eats two Big Macs, Juliet is no longer hungry.

Each of these events is dependent on the event that happened before, snowballing into this story. This causal relationship between events, with the character being the driving force, is essential for plots. Now, do stories ever have hurricanes rush through town, causing many events that the character or characters couldn't have been at the heart of? Absolutely! This often speaks to the genre you're writing within. Getting more familiar with the expectations within your selected genre will help you decide if your plot will be purely character-driven, or if events beyond a character's control will also have an impact on your story.

FIND THE PLOT

Time to find the plot from familiar books, movies, and/or plays! What happens in the stories you are familiar with? How does one event cause the next event? And what relationship does that have with the characters and their objectives?

- Pick a play or movie that you are familiar with.
- Starting with the beginning of the story, name each event in the **plot**.
    - Write these out in your notebook.
- Once you have all the events noted, ask yourself:
    - What is the relationship between each event?
    - What relationships do these events have with the **characters** and their **objectives**?
- Repeat as much as is helpful with another movie or play.
- If you're in a group, have volunteers share.

FIRST CRACK AT YOUR STRUCTURE

Writing Cue ❯❯

Now that you have a better handle on structure, let's think about what shape your play will take! You will need to decide if your story will be following a single character (protagonist) or a group of characters (ensemble), what they want, and how their journey to get their want affects them and everyone else in your story. You can either set a timer with at least fifteen to twenty minutes, or don't let yourself stop until you have your structure. You will need:

- **A springboard** for the story you wish to tell.
- The **genre** and/or **subgenre** this story fits in.
- The **time** and **place** of your story, also known as its setting.
- A good idea of the **characters** you wish to include, at the bare minimum a protagonist, or the ensemble, depending on which you'll be using.
- Each **character's objective**.
- What **conflict** and **obstacles** stand in the way of your **characters** reaching their **objectives**.
- What is at **stake** for your **character**, or ensemble, should they fail or succeed.

Get your timer ready, or just settle into tackling all of these points. This can be written out in paragraphs, or bullet points. I'm quite partial to outlines with bullet points, but I encourage you to tackle this in the form that feels the most comfortable for you. Try not to think too much. Remember, this sketch of your structure is a first draft and can be changed before you jump into writing your play.

Ready? GO!

FIRST CRACK AT YOUR PLOT

Writing Cue ≫

Now let's tackle the plot of this play. Using the structure you just completed, start thinking about what events will get you from the beginning of your play to the end, and what the relationship between them, and your characters' objectives, will be. Again, you can either give yourself fifteen to twenty minutes on a timer, or just sit down and crank out your plot until you reach the end. Take the structure you just sketched out and add:

- The first event of the story—think about what caused it.
- What happens next because of this first event and how your **character** reacted to it?
- Keep going, trying to keep each event or point driven by the previous event and/or the **character's** reaction to it.
- Keep in mind the **macro-objective** of the play.
    - What **micro-objectives** can build to this **macro-objective**?
- Think about what stands in your **characters'** way, what **actions** your **characters** might take to get around those **obstacles**, and what events are caused by those **actions**.
- Think of dominos and snowballs.

This is a first draft, be patient with yourself and your writing muscles. And again, there's no right or wrong form these plot points can take. Let them come out and live on the page in the most natural way for you. Ready? GO!

❮ Interval ❯

- Stop writing once the timer goes off.
- Stand, stretch, move, shake it out.
- How did that feel?
    - Were there any surprises? Unexpected turns?
- Do you feel like you know your characters better?
- Do you feel like you know the story you want to tell better?
- Are you itching to start writing your play?
    - Or are you more confused than ever?
- If you're in a group, have volunteers share sections of their structures and/or plots.

WHEN TO IGNORE YOUR PLANS

You are so almost ready to start your play! Woo-hoo! You have done so much hard work, and so much careful planning. Does that mean you are forever married to every decision you made in your predraft work? 100 percent no!

These sketches are there, like nets below a tightrope walker, to help you when you miss a step or fall. But I encourage you to let your characters be your ultimate guide on this journey. I often sketch out my structure and plot, only to immediately be faced with a character that has different ideas. When this happens, this is that inner writer trying to come out. I always *always* let it. Even if it means I need to re-sketch out everything. Remember, you invented the world, but your characters live there. Let them take you down unexpected rabbit holes. If they surprise you, it's more likely they will surprise your audience. These sketches are more for when you sit down to write the next scene and you're not feeling completely confident about what happens next. When your characters aren't quite ready to grab your hand and take you on their next adventure.

As always, everything written can be changed. You might find that the path your character took you down doesn't work for the play, but that's actually amazing news. The more you know what is and isn't your play, the more you understand what you want your play to be. So let your characters wander, and follow along to see where they lead. Nothing is set in stone, and every journey gives you something to learn.

SPOTLIGHT ON STRUCTURE AND PLOT

Maybe after writing your outline you feel pumped and ready to write your play. Maybe that was hard and painful and you feel more lost and confused. Maybe you're somewhere in between. All of those feelings are correct. In my writing process, sketching and outlining structure and plot tends to be the most taxing on my brain and creative juices. Sometimes I go through all of these steps and my hands are just itching to start writing dialogue, with everything feeling natural and easy as butter. Other times it's like pulling teeth and I hate my sketches and my characters and feel utterly lost. I've written successful plays coming from both of these places. Just because it's easy doesn't mean the play is going to be good, and just because it's hard doesn't mean the idea is terrible and you should chuck the whole thing.

Playwright Edward Albee said that every time you start a new play, it's like you have to learn how to write plays all over again. And he's not wrong. Every play is its own beast coming with its own ease and/or complications. It's like my example of hiking through the woods from the chapter on springboards. Sometimes a hike is flat and ends at a waterfall and along the way you see baby deer and bunnies, and sometimes it's uphill and too hot and filled with biting insects, and there's a fallen tree blocking you from seeing the amazing view you worked so hard to see, and as you stomp your way back down the mountain, you find a napping full-grown adult moose blocking your path back to civilization. Both of these hikes will make you a better hiker. Every hike makes you a better hiker. And you don't know which hike will turn into the most amazing story later when you're reliving it for friends. Plays are the same way. Every play will make you a stronger writer. Every draft. Every outline. Every brainstorming list, even.

Moving forward, try to identify the structure and plot of every book you pick up to read, movie you sit down to watch, or play you either sit down to watch or read. These observations will strengthen your understanding and give you clarity on future stories you wish to tell.

BEGINNINGS

GET PUMPED, IT'S TIME to start your play! Armed with our **springboard**, choice of **genre** and/or **subgenre**, the **time** and **place** your play will take place, the **characters**, and your handy-dandy **structure** and **plot** outline, let's break pages on something brand new. It's probably my most and least favorite part of writing. I know that's a contradiction, but writing is nothing if not a contradiction. At least for me.

So we're starting this play, what do we do now? Let's walk through the basics of what most plays have in the beginning, so we know what to expect when we get going.

STAGE DIRECTIONS

Stage Directions are the words in a script that explain what is happening onstage. Remember, movies tell stories through pictures, and plays tell stories through dialogue, but another piece of the play puzzle is the actions that must happen in order to tell the story. We use stage directions not only to describe what our stage looks like, and when our characters move, exit, or enter, but also to set the tone for the script, giving a deeper sense of the world we've created.

When I first started writing for the stage, every time a character needed to actually physically do something, I would be stopped in my tracks. But stage directions don't need to be an intimidating force. We can harness stage directions and turn them into the ultimate authority in this story and this world. Remember, your script is a blueprint. Once you've written and rewritten (and maybe rewritten ten more times), your play will hopefully go off to get produced. Everything in your script informs your production team and actors on how to bring your play to life, and stage directions make that blueprint all the more clear.

So, what *is* essential to include in the stage directions? If it has to happen for the story to make sense, but it's not conveyed in dialogue, you must include it in your stage directions. Here's a handy-dandy list of potentially essential stage directions:

1. Description of Setting

All that fun time and place stuff. Where are we? When are we? As you practice and write more, you will get a better feeling for how much detail you'd like to go into in order to paint the picture for your audience.

Examples from my published plays:

> *Just before midnight. The basement of the Red House, a filthy place. There are boxes and jars with strange liquids in every corner. An old bed sits in the middle with a small skeleton on it. The half-decomposed body of an enormous dog is on the floor. There is a terrible rotten smell that the audience can see.* (*The Red House Monster*)

> *The Pack Horse Library Project Center of Breathitt County, located in a back room of a church. There are shelves with lots of books, and a long central table.*
>
> *The set should be simple and implied. It'll change a lot, and too much stuff will slow the transitions. Let the audience fill in what you don't physically show them. The few set pieces should be multi-taskers ready to become many different things in all of our various settings.* (*The Book Women*)

2. Character Entrances and Exits

This one is important. It helps your readers track who is onstage and who isn't, and later will inform your director and their blocking.

Examples from my published plays:

JUNO enters, nonplussed and disgruntled. She drags her backpack like an obstinate pet. (*The Hardy Girls*)

MERE snaps her fingers, FILLE and GARCON exit, then enter with costumes needing mending, they each make many trips and pile so much on top of IRO that by time they're done we no longer see IRO. (*Of Serpents and Sea Spray*)

3. Character Descriptions

These can be physical descriptions, mood descriptions, both, or neither. You're trying to give enough information to your reader so that they get a sense of the character. This doesn't need, and shouldn't, be a full history. Allow for discoveries to be made throughout the play.

Here are a couple of examples from some of my published plays:

SANTA, he/him, jolly with a belly full of jelly. Wears a lot of red.

KRAMPUS, he/him, eerie with a belly full of puss. Wears a dirty cloak made out of badgers. (From the character list of *Santa's Old Friend*, in the collection *Holly, Jolly, and Extra Folly*)

There's a knock on the door. ERMA answers. LEO BURNET enters with a suitcase and photography equipment. It's a lot of stuff. LEO's clothes don't look like they were meant to be covered in dust, which they very much are. (*The Book Women*)

4. Essential Physical Actions

What physical actions are absolutely essential? A slap? A kiss? Shredding incriminating documents? What actions absolutely have to happen?

Examples from my published plays:

MARA rips the sleeves off of her shirt. Her arms are covered in fur as are her hands. Instead of nails she has claws. (*I Said Run*, in the collection *It's Her Say*)

JENNIFER yawns, then takes out a cookbook and a large mixing bowl and starts to make the dough for rolls. She yawns, then slaps her face, trying to keep alert. She measures flour. She yawns again. She gets close to the book to read the next instruction and falls asleep in the book . . . (*Mom's Ham*, in the collection *Holly, Jolly, and Extra Folly*)

Because the stage directions are literally the words of the creator (you), make every word count. In my comedies I often make jokes in my stage directions, though only essential jokes of course. Stage Directions are another way for you to show where we are and the feeling of that place. An audience will never know what the stage directions say, instead a production team will take those directions and give the audience the information through their specialties. So, while the audience doesn't get to see the stage directions that say "a summer's morning," they get the idea of morning through the lighting design, and idea of summer from the costumes the characters wear and an actor fanning themselves.

Beyond just the information of what's happening onstage, you also get to set the tone with your stage directions. You must use every single chance you have to make your play distinct and engaging. What is this play? What feelings are you hoping to evoke? I don't mean that you need to make "*JULIET exits*" into a joke, but when the opportunity presents itself, don't let it pass you by.

EXPOSITION

Our characters want things, but as your characters talk, it's good to know that going after their objective isn't the only thing you need from the words coming out of their mouths . . . You also need to give information to your audience. Almost everything that you need your audience to know in order to understand your story will come from the words spoken by your characters. What is this world? Who are these people? What do they want? Why are we here? Information said out loud by our characters is called exposition, and typically there's a lot of exposition in the beginning of a play.

The tricky part of exposition is knowing when there isn't enough and knowing how much is too much. Finding that happy balance comes with practice. It's also why I read my scripts out loud to myself sitting alone in my office. When I'm reading, I ask myself: is this how normal people talk? Unless, of course, I'm not going for the genre of realism in this play. Which gets back to the importance of having some idea of where you want your play to eventually fit in the world. In a farce, for example, you often deliver information in an abundantly obvious manner for comedic effect.

When I first started writing, one of the traps I kept falling into was trying to give all the information right out of the gate. Lucky for us all, you don't need to do that. You have an entire play to give out those essential details. Realizing that you don't need everything up front does two things: it gives you space to relax because you no longer have the pressure of telling an entire life story in the first ten pages, and it also makes your eventual audience lean in. They're curious about why the brother and sister are fighting so much. Or why the word "aspiration" is met with such disdain from the uncle. If you give an audience space to wonder, you can make them hungry for information, as opposed to being overwhelmed by it.

FIND THE EXPOSITION

The next time you sit down to read a script, underline the information it gives you about the story. You can find exposition in both the stage directions and the spoken words of dialogue. I want you to especially notice the exposition from the words said out loud. For how long in the play is the playwright giving information? What is the tone of this information?

As with stage directions, and all those Act One tools, looking at the exposition in the plays you read can sharpen your understanding of exposition, making you more confident about how and when you dole out all of that essential information in your own work.

LET ME SHOW YOU THE WORLD

Now that we know how to set the stage (literally, with stage directions), and how information is given through dialogue and stage directions (exposition), let's talk about the very,

very beginning of your play. Remember from the chapter on structure, you build the world before you flip the world on its head with your inciting incident. Normally you have the first 10 percent of your play to do this. After all, flipping a world upside down doesn't always hit if we, as the audience, don't realize it's been flipped. Do you always have to follow this rule? Absolutely not. As always, you're the boss. But I think it helps to know the rules so you understand when you're bending or breaking them. Also, this is another one of those yummy parameters. The less we have to decide for ourselves, the easier all this writing gets.

So the first 10 percent is what we have to work with: in a ten-minute play, this is about one page; in a forty-five-minute play, this is about four or five pages; and in a full-length play that's between eighty and one hundred minutes, this is about eight to ten pages. In those pages, we should give some information on the following:

- Where we are (**place**)
- When we are (**time**)
- Who we are (**characters**)
- What the rules of this world are
- Why we should care
- What the characters want

Do we have to share everything? Absolutely not. We learned in the section on exposition that patience can be our friend. Think of this instead as a light sketch for the audience, which you'll fill in with color and detail as the play continues.

SHOW ME YOUR WORLD

Writing Cue ❯❯

The time is finally here! I'm excited, are you excited? Let's break pages on your play! I want you to write the opening pages of your play, introducing the world, the people, the objectives, and any details you think are essential. Remember, this doesn't have to be good. These pages can be ridiculous. They can be trash garbage. It's not important what these pages are in the beginning. What's important is that they go from ideas in your brain to the page.

Arm yourself with your outline and sketch. Remember the rules of the genre you want this play to belong to, and the rules of structure you're going to follow or ignore. Pick all of that up into your brain, give it a good long squeeze, and then release. We're going to *not* think again. We're going to just let the words happen, knowing that rewriting exists for a reason, and we can't rewrite until we have a messy first draft to work with.

As always, do not, do not, do not worry about grammar or punctuation! For this exercise, you will need:

- Writing utensils
- Your **springboard**
- Your **genre** and/or **subgenre**
- Your **characters**
- Your **time**
- Your **place**
- Your characters' **objectives**
- A willingness to let all of this go as your hands start to work

You won't have a timer this time. You will write until you feel like you've set up this world. Ready? GO!

❮ Interval ❯

- Stop writing once you've introduced your characters and world.
- Stand, stretch, move, shake it out.
    - If you need more movement, do it. Maybe you need a walk, or a sixty-second dance party, or a cup of your favorite coffee drink, or something else entirely. Reward yourself. You just did a hard thing!
- How did that feel?
    - Did anything surprise you?
    - What was easier than you expected?
    - What was harder?
- Read your setup out loud to yourself, or if you're in a group, have volunteers share.
    - Identify:
        - Where we are
        - When we are
        - Who the characters are
        - What the characters want
        - What is the characters' way
- **OR: Don't read or share yet.** I know we've been reading and sharing this whole time, but when I'm in a brand-new first draft I will wait until I've finished the draft before I go

back and read anything. It helps me feel urgency to get to the end before I go back, but that might not work for you. The only way you'll know is to try everything, and then hold onto what feeds your specific craft.

INCITING INCIDENT

We've built the world—who's ready to turn it on its head? The inciting incident is about to change everything. When I was in grad school, I was told to ask myself the Passover question at the beginning of any play: how is this night different from all other nights?

We know where and when this world is, we know the characters, we know some of the rules. But why is this play happening right now? It's because something is about to happen that is different than anything these characters, or this world, have experienced. Everything changes.

In the world-building of *Hamlet* we learn:

- That a ghost has been haunting the castle.
- That the old king, Hamlet's father, is dead.
- That the queen, Hamlet's mother, married the king's brother within a month of the old king's death, making Hamlet's uncle the new king.
- That Hamlet is super angry about this hasty marriage, and is in the midst of experiencing agonizing grief from the death of his father.

And then, Act One, Scene Five happens and we get the inciting incident:

- Hamlet meets with the ghost and learns:
    - This ghost is the ghost of his father, the old king.
    - The old king's death wasn't natural, it was murder.
    - The old king was murdered by his brother, the new king.
    - The old king wants Hamlet to avenge his death and kill the new king.

Hamlet's world is flipped upside down and he is set on his journey.

FIND THE INCITING INCIDENT

Classic plays are excellent places to look for inciting incidents, but modern plays have them too! As do books, movies, and TV shows. Think over your favorites and identify what incident sets the characters in motion. Set a timer for fifteen minutes and try to identify as many inciting incidents as you can. If you want a challenge, limit yourself only to work meant for the stage.

- Look over your list:
    - How are these inciting incidents different from one another?
    - How are they similar?
- If you're in a group, have volunteers share examples.

Writing Cue ❯❯

Take your opening pages from the world-building exercise and keep going. Turn the world upside down and shake it around like a kid catching insects in a jar does to see if any of the insects will start a battle. We need to set things on fire, or our characters will have nothing to work to fix, or break even further. You should have an idea of what this incident is from your sketch/outline from the chapter on structure and plot. If that no longer works, throw it out! Remember: how is this night different from all other nights?

You will need:

- Your beginning pages that built your world and characters.
- An event that shatters everything you just built.

No timer. Just sit down, write, and finish when the event is over.

Try not to think.

Try only to write.

Ready? GO!

❮ Interval ❯

- Once you've written the full inciting incident, and likely left your world and characters devastated, stop writing.
- Stand, stretch, move, shake it out.
    - Like with the world-building writing cue, you may need more than a stretch—after all, you just flipped an entire world upside down. Indulge yourself.
- How did that feel?
    - Did anything surprise you?

    - What was easier than you expected?
    - What was harder?
- As you did with world-building, read your inciting incident out loud, or don't. This is where you can start to work out what works best for your craft. The same applies if you're working in a group. Is it helpful for writers to share? Or do they want to get to the end before they hear their work? There is no wrong answer.

SPOTLIGHT ON BEGINNINGS

You now have the beginning of your play! Congratulations! Let yourself feel good about getting the words out. Even if you're not confident in them. Especially if you're not confident in them. Writing is hard. Bad writing is merely a step on the way to rewriting, which is where we find better writing.

Moving forward, pay attention to the beginnings of stories. Remember, as writers, we don't just get to passively enjoy stories anymore—we get to be stronger writers by dissecting the work that's already living in the world. Take notes on beginnings that you find particularly gripping. Maybe the inciting incident literally blows the world up, or maybe it's quiet and subtle. A quiet shake is still a shake. The trick is finding the shake, or flip, or fire, or explosion that works for your play right now. When in doubt? Pick one and go for it. If it doesn't work, that's what rewriting is for.

MIDDLES

WE HAVE THE BEGINNING of our play! Woo-hoo! Now all we need to do is write everything that happens in the middle of the play. Which, as it happens, is the vast majority of the play. Everything after the inciting incident, but before the climax, is the middle. So what happens next? That's up to you. Your characters go on wanting things, little micro-objectives throughout each of your scenes, which feed the large macro-objective that they're moving toward in the climax. This can feel like the writing slog. Writing the world-building and inciting incident is first up in the process, when we're bright-eyed and bushy-tailed. This is where you, the writer, can start to feel haggard, and lost in the weeds.

In this section I'm going to show you how I move through the middle of the play, slow and steady just like the Little Engine that Could.

GOALS AND DEADLINES

I love goals, and I love deadlines. Does that mean that every time I sit down to write I'm meeting my goals? Absolutely not. Am I always meeting deadlines? Nope. Then why am I such a fan? I am a sucker for structure in every aspect of my writing. And deadlines and goals give me structure in how I move through a new play.

Writing is an alone game most of the time. We are writing for theatre, so eventually we get lovely actors, designers, and a director to work with, but you're still going to be alone a lot, especially in writing a first draft. Just you and your chosen writing tool and blank pages. Without writing goals or deadlines, that can start to feel a bit like being set adrift on a raft in the ocean. So I give myself goals and I set deadlines, to tether me to something. My goals and deadlines have shifted over the years as I get to know and better understand my writing process, but I still get thrown for a loop sometimes, and miss a goal and come out late on a deadline. While I think it's tremendously important to have both goals and deadlines, it is just as important to be kind to ourselves when we don't make it. Dream big, but remember, it isn't the end of the world if it takes longer than expected.

When you set off writing your first play, you may not really know how much you'll write, or when you should expect to finish. And that's okay! Even with this unknown, I urge you to give yourself a timeline. This could look like:

- Writing for one hour every day.
- Writing one scene every other day.
- Writing at least ten pages every Friday.

Knowing if you work best with time-based goals, scene-completion goals, page goals, or some other type of goal altogether is something you'll learn as you go. I write with scene goals in mind. I will give myself anywhere from one to three scenes to finish in one day, using my hand-dandy outline to get me over any humps or hiccups I face along the way. I would recommend picking one type of goal for this project, and when you start in on your next play, try something new.

I'm about to ask you to start sketching out your writing goals and deadlines, but before we do that, know that often writing feels like the last thing you actually want to do. These goals and deadlines are there so you can tell yourself, OKAY, this might be hard but I only have five pages to write today, or one scene, or whatever you've set for yourself. The more you reach those goals, the better you will feel. If you find the goals are really getting away from you and that first-draft deadline you set for yourself is coming on way too fast like a bullet train, there is an easy fix . . . Adjust your plan! That's the beautiful thing. Just make sure you have a plan that keeps you writing regularly, but stretch it out for as long as you need.

WRITING PLAN!

Writing Cue ➤➤

Let's make a plan. If you have a reason this plan needs to be done by a certain time, like for class or a competition, I would work backward from there, giving yourself at least a couple of days for wiggle room. Looking over your outlines, how much time will you need for each bullet point? If you have no idea, just guess, and be prepared to adjust when it's either too demanding or not challenging enough. In your plan, be as specific as possible, and be sure you think about all of the things in your life:

- When will you have time to write regularly?
- How much time will you have?
- Factor in your other obligations like school, the job that financially supports you, or caregiving.
- Feel free to start small, with little blocks of writing time, and build up as your writing muscles grow.

For your plan, I highly recommend either writing it on your computer or on loose paper. You'll see why in a sec. This is what you need to answer:

- How much do you expect to write every session (writing goal)?
- When do you expect to be finished (deadline)?

If you are addicted to having a timer, give yourself at least five or ten minutes. Ready to write down your plan? Great! GO!

❮ Interval ❯

- Once you've mapped out all your goals and deadlines to finish this draft, stop! If you're using a timer, hopefully you've finished by the time it goes off. If not, be sure to finish!
- Stand, stretch, move, shake it out.
- Print out your plan if you wrote on a laptop. If not, go straight to posting your plan near where you will be sitting down to write. Somewhere you can see it.
    - I love crossing off or checking off each goal on my writing plan. It gives me an inordinate amount of joy. I'm all about celebrating the little victories along the way.

KEEP MOVING FORWARD

As you start to write and write, adjusting your plan as needed in your process, remember to keep moving forward. It's tempting to pull out your writing tools and start rewriting your beginning before you write any new pages. Beware this temptation! It can keep you stuck in scene one for an eternity. And really, you won't know what the beginning *has* to be until you've written all the way to the end.

So! In your notebook or on your computer, try your very best to keep moving ahead in your script until you reach that end. For your hard work and diligence, you will be rewarded with an entire play to tinker with! Which, I can tell you, is a lot more fun than tinkering with only one scene of a play. So forward, my friends! Always forward!

WHEN YOU'RE STUCK

Sometimes the middle of a first draft can feel like a slog. Characters lose interest, writers get bored, resolutions wane. But never fear, all of that is a natural part in the writing process. For example, as I write the *middle* of this very book, I have to fight the urge to chuck my computer out the window every other day. It can be rough, but this is the time to lean into the *play* aspect of your play.

We said right from the start that there's a reason why they're called *plays*. They're pretend! They can be out-of-this-world wild. They absolutely do not have to make sense. Whenever I am stuck and feeling stagnant in my plans or characters, I shake things up by throwing something absolutely wild into the mix. Maybe a twenty-foot-high iguana stomps through the town, knocking down a house or two. Maybe your protagonist wins the lottery! The point is, even if the idea is terrible or outlandish, sometimes you need to shake stuff up big time to get to the end of draft one, and that is okay! After all, you're writing none of this in stone. So when you need to burn the school down in order to shake your protagonist to actually finish their journey, the important part is that they're at the finish line. Take out the iguana or fire later, but for now, spice things up enough to keep you interested so you actually get to that amazing moment when you get to write: *End of Play.*

STILL STUCK? THAT'S WHY WE HAVE A TOOLBOX!

If the giant iguana didn't get things moving in your draft, go back to the first section of the book, back to those tools we put in our toolbox:

Objective

- What does my character want?
    - What happens if I make the objective bigger?
    - What happens if I make the objective smaller?

Action

- What is my character doing to reach their objective?
- What haven't they tried?
- What could they try again with new and improved tools?

Stakes

- What is on the line for my characters?
- Do the stakes change throughout the play?
- What happens to my characters when the stakes get bigger?
- What happens to my characters when the stakes get smaller?

Conflict

- Who is standing in my characters' way?
- How can they convince them to move?
- What happens when they lose?
- What happens when they win?

Obstacle

- What is standing in my characters' way that can't be moved?
- Is there a way around?
- Is a sacrifice required?

Tactics

- What actions haven't my characters tried?
    - When do they need to try something new?
    - How many new things can they try?
        - Is this helping or hurting their cause?
- When do my characters refuse to change tactics?
    - Why?
        - Is this helping or hurting their cause?

Just like when we got silly with these tools in Act One, they're around for you to get silly with again while you're trying to get this first draft done. They're also ready to get serious. Take any exercise that grabbed you from Act One and use those instructions for the next scene of your play. Let's say you're writing a scene where two characters need to make a decision together, but you're not sure how to make that exciting . . . having a specific action for each character might help. Flip back to the action exercises, pick one, then proceed using your current project's circumstances. Or, maybe you want your protagonist to attack their objective more ferociously—jump back to the stakes exercises and pick the one that strums up inspiration. It's okay if it doesn't make total sense. You can work all of that out later, the point is to keep on moving, keep on grooving, by any means necessary.

SPOTLIGHT ON MIDDLES

Write and write and write and write and write and write and write! Did I mention you should write? There are no wrong answers in first drafts—that's the best thing about them. The middle is just the thing that you need to get through in order to end your story.

In my first draft of *The Book Women*, I stuck pretty closely to my original outline. The characters of the four packhorse librarians each came out bright and shiny and very distinct from one another, while the reporter from New York was elusive. Every time I had a scene to write with Leo Burnet, it was a slog. Unlike the librarians, he was bland and vague. But I made myself push through the draft, and wrote each scene I had planned out as it came up on my schedule, even though I knew one of the characters needed a tremendous amount of work. First drafts are there to be painful and ridiculous, and yes, sometimes even boring. I knew that I could worry over that character after the play actually existed. And later, in rewriting, I got to change it! Through finishing the first draft, I had the head space needed to make Leo Burnet unique and specific.

So go forth and write. Have a character that doesn't excite you. Repeat lines. Let loose giant iguanas. Set the town on fire. Changing it later is a lot easier than writing it now.

ENDINGS

WOW, WOW, WOW! WE'RE HERE! The end of your play! Congratulations! It is incredibly hard to write an entire play, and you are one ending away from doing just that. Maybe you've been following all those plans you wrote out to every last detail, or maybe your characters took you on a wild goose chase and you've had to throw out every plan you made along the way. Either way, you're here! The end of the play! So now that you're here, what's the ending?

EVERYTHING ACCORDING TO PLAN

I had you do a lot of work before you started this first draft, and in the course of mapping out structure and plot, you should have generated at least one idea of how your play *could* end. If you've been following that outline, and so far everything has been working just the way you imagined it, keep going! There is nothing at all wrong with continuing to follow a plan. Sometimes our brains are able to lay stories all out on the table, and sometimes they get details wrong. If you got your plan right from the beginning, don't panic! There is nothing wrong with correctly predicting all the twists and turns of a story.

WHEN PLANS FAIL

We've all been there. I've been there. You thought up everything so carefully, but when you sit down to write the thing, your char-

acters go off in surprising directions and getting them to follow your carefully plotted-out plot is more challenging than herding two dozen cats. If your characters won't stick to the plan, feel free to also chuck it out the window. Because in addition to having you write out your outline, I also had you think about the genre of your play. This is one of those parameter gifts. Looking at genre, you know how plays like yours *typically* end. If you don't know how else to end your play, go back to what has worked for so many, many stories before yours. After all, if it's not broken, why fix it?

If leaning into genre isn't helping, my next go-to is: get silly. After all, a twenty-foot iguana stepping on your protagonist would probably be both unexpected and incredibly final. So go big! Trust me when I tell you that finishing the play is more important at this point than getting the ending right. First drafts are not in the business of getting many things right. So get big, get weird, get silly, and get to the end of your play.

If silly ideas are in short supply, or if you'd like to give it one last go at finishing your draft in the same lane as you started it, my next go-to is brainstorming.

BRAINSTORMING WHEN PLANS FAIL

❮ Interval ❯

When one plan fails, you can always brainstorm up a new one. You're at the end, and not one of your characters is cooperating, and you just need to finish this draft, but how to go about that? Get your timers ready. Give yourself at least fifteen minutes OR give yourself a very big number of options to write, at least fifty. You'll want as many options as possible.

Get in a comfortable position with your writing tools of choice. When you're set, list all the possible endings that you could use.

These can get very silly, and please let them. Remember, you have to let all sorts of ideas fall out of your brain before you get useful ones sometimes. Don't think, just write! Ready? GO!

Once you're done with your brainstormed list, look through all of your options. If none jump out to you as the obvious solution, pick the option you dislike the least.

WRITE AN ENDING, ANY ENDING

Writing Cue ❯❯

Have your space set up, comfortable seat, good lighting—the whole nine yards. When everything works for you, sit down and write. Write until the story has been completed. Let it be weird, let it take too long, let it happen too fast. This is a MESSY first draft, and that absolutely includes the ending. When you finally do get to the end, your reward is getting to write the three words that playwrights love above all others: END OF PLAY.

Ready to do this? Great!

WRITE THAT ENDING!

❮ Interval ❯

Stretch! Your hands, your back, your arms, your legs, your toes, your fingers, your neck. Stretch it all. Go for a walk. Or a run. Eat a treat. All of the above? You bet. You did it. You have a first draft of your play! Please treat yourself in some way, big or small, because this is a big accomplishment, and we must train our inner writer to feel good when it finishes a first draft.

- How did it feel?

    - Was anything easier than you expected before you began?
    - Was anything more complicated than expected?
- Now you can go back to the beginning of your play!
- Either read your entire play out loud to yourself, by yourself, like I do, or invite over some actors or friends. I find that pizza always helps this invitation.
- If you're already in a classroom or a writers' group, have volunteers share their drafts!
    - Before you listen to the play, be very clear on if you'd like feedback on the draft, and if you do, outline guidelines on how feedback should be given. If you just want to hear the play, and don't want feedback, that is also perfectly okay! You drive the bus.
        - I will go over feedback in more detail in Act Three, but in the meantime, I can't recommend Liz Lerman's Critical Response Process enough! The reason I love it is that it puts the artist in the driver's seat and stays clear of opinions until the very end, and then they're optional! Receiving feedback is another muscle you will build as a writer—don't tax it too much by bombarding yourself with too many outside opinions.

SPOTLIGHT ON ENDINGS

Phew! Wow! You did it! And you might have even heard your whole play out loud by now! Well done. It is hard to write a first draft—they often come out so messy and oddly shaped. You should feel good no matter what shape your draft is in.

My most ridiculous first-draft ending was in my play *Burst,* where I had an FBI agent bust down the door and start arresting all of my characters. I just didn't know what else to do. But I needed to get the first draft done. And it gave all of my friends a big hearty laugh when they gathered to read it out loud for me. AND, even more importantly, after hearing it, I realized that it couldn't be the ending for *Burst.* I learned that *Burst* wasn't that type of play. The next ending I wrote in rewrites? That's how *Burst* is supposed to end. And I never would have gotten there without forcing myself to end that first draft by any means necessary.

... Intermission ...

We've finished Act Two! Well done!

In Act One, not only did we learn tricks on how to **unleash** our inner writers, we also filled a toolbox to the brim with dramatic tools: **objective**, **action**, **stakes**, **conflict**, **obstacle**, and **tactics**. In Act Two, we sketched all the specific elements of your play: **springboard**, **genre**, **time** and **place**, **characters**, **structure** and **plot**, and then created a new play with the chapters on **beginnings**, **middles**, and **endings**. My hope is that by now you not only have a fully written (messy) first draft, but also all the tools you will need to rework that play into the play you want it to be.

Act One and Act Two were a lot of work. You should feel very proud of getting this far and putting in so much effort. Need a break? This is the time to do that. Get in a good stretch, go on a walk, listen to your favorite song, or even treat yourself to a night out at a theater!

As we now move forward to the third and final act, you may be wondering what we possibly have left to build. After all, we've built our writer's toolbox and an entire play! What could be next? Well, now we're going to be building a playwright. Someone capable of not only finishing one first draft, but also picking up that draft and reworking it, and then starting a new project and going through the whole process again. Welcome to Act Three, where we dive deeper into *craft*.

Act Three
BUILDING A PLAYWRIGHT

WROUGHT

HAVE YOU EVER THOUGHT about why it's "play**wright**" instead of "playwriter"? It's because plays are **wrought**, like iron. Created with precision and strength and fortitude. A forging of words. We hold the hammer in this process, often beginning alone and then gaining input from actors, directors, designers, and audiences, to get the play to its most essential. In the following pages, we'll talk about forging, and how to hone not only your plays, but also how to hone your inner writer so you can become the most essential playwright you can be.

My acting teacher Coach taught me that my body, mind, and soul make up my acting instrument. And, much like a saxophone player must take great care with their saxophone, we must always take care with our instrument as well. What stretches do my limbs need to keep me limber? What exercises to keep my muscles strong? Am I reading enough? Am I watching enough? How is my listening? How is my voice?

Moving from acting to writing, I brought these lessons into this new craft. How can I stretch my playwriting instrument? Make it stronger? Make it grow? Being a playwright is a lifetime of figuring out what your instrument needs. Which hammers to use, and how hot the fire needs to be for continuous learning and development. I structure my creative life around the following tenets. Keep what helps you. Throw out what doesn't. And then go out and discover more.

REWRITING

YOU HAVE THAT FIRST DRAFT and you're thinking, "I did the hard thing. Now what?" Now we **rewrite**. How one does that is very personal for every playwright. Part of building yourself as a playwright is figuring out what works for you.

NEXT STEPS

My next step after a first draft tends to be one of these two things:

- I read the entire play out loud to myself in my office. I'll read through my larger-cast plays multiple times, so I can focus on only a few characters at a time.
- OR I invite over actor friends, and they read it out loud for me, as I listen along with the script and a red pen at the ready.

Whether I'm reading aloud or actors are, I'm listening for a number of things, including but not limited to:

- What's confusing? What doesn't make sense?
- Do all of the characters' journeys, emotional or otherwise, make sense?
- Does my attention wander at any point? When does the play lag?

- And the opposite of that—where are there jumps too big to follow?
- Does the dialogue feel natural? Or, if not natural, in line with the genre I'm going for?
- Where are people laughing?
- Where are people feeling feelings? Did anyone cry?
- Do my characters feel like real people? Or again, if not real, in line with the genre?
- Is there enough tension and conflict to keep an audience interested for the play's length?
- What is the play currently doing right now?
    - How is it currently functioning?
    - How do I *want* it to function?

As I listen, I mark the script up with symbols, scribbles, and notes. I star sections I like. I draw a smiley face when the play makes me, or anyone in the room, laugh. I scratch out text I want to lose. I write words like "MORE!" when I think things jump too fast from one moment to another. After hearing the first draft, I go back in, armed with my notes, and start rewriting.

HOW IS THE PLAY CURRENTLY FUNCTIONING?

What's on the page right now? It helps to take the judgment out of rewriting. Instead of telling yourself, "The second half of the play is garbage and I want to throw it into the sea," try: "The second half of the play has a lot of pauses in the dialogue, which creates a lot of air and a slow pace in the text." It's hard to rewrite something you've written off as terrible. But, if you attack it from a function standpoint, you set yourself into a more neutral position. And the more we practice analyzing both our own work and the work of others, the stronger that skill will become. Remember those many "Find the X" sections? We'll now turn those analytic skills we've been developing onto our own work.

What can you find in your play right now?

- What are the **objectives**?
- What are your characters' **actions**?
- What is at **stake**?
- Where's the **conflict**?
- Where are the **obstacles**?
- What different **tactics** are taken?
- Where does the play embrace the **genre/subgenre**?
- Where does the play defy the **genre/subgenre**?
- What is the **setting**?
- What does the **structure** look like?
    - Where do we go on your characters' journey?
    - Where do we end up?
- Is the relevant information given in **stage directions**?
    - Is there ever too much information?
    - Is there ever not enough information?
- How is your **exposition** delivered?

HOW DO I WANT THE PLAY TO FUNCTION?

Function gets to the heart of what your play is, and you can measure this current functionality against how you want it to function, and then start to play with your play. Remember Act One? Rewriting is why we learned about those tools for our toolbox. Does a scene not have enough drama? Play with stakes. Is a character kinda aimless? Play with objectives. Does a scene feel stagnant? Play with tactics. Does it feel too easy for your protagonist? Play with obstacles.

As you tinker and play, everything can always be changed. None of this is set in stone. There are no rules saying you can't go back to an older draft. Figuring out which tool to use takes practice, and sometimes you'll need to use more than one tool. Much like with first drafts, you get the hang of it with practice. So take your opening scene where nothing happens and look back on the chapter about action. Are there any physical actions you brainstormed that can make the scene more dynamic? Play around! And keep playing until your draft functions the way you want it to.

MY REWRITING PROCESS

To date, I have seventeen full-length plays that I let other people see. An undisclosed number live in a secret folder on my computer, never to see the light of day. Of the seventeen I share with the world, twelve of them have received at least one full production, and ten of them are published. How did I move from draft one to the world premiere? World premiere to publication? Each play has a different journey, but many share a similar path. Usually my process goes something like:

1. First draft.
2. Me, alone in my office, reading out all of the dialogue and stage directions, correcting anything that bugs me along the way. This step is often repeated. Once I've gotten to the point where I think it could not be any better, I have:
3. Draft 1.5.
    - For some reason, I can't think of it as a second draft if I'm the only one who's read it.
4. Table reading with readers who are not me.
    - This might be my friends, who I'll buy pizza for.
    - This might be students at one of the nearby colleges or youth theaters I regularly work with.
    - This might be actors at a theatre company I have a relationship with.
5. Take a million notes when hearing the play, plus a million more notes from the discussion after hearing the play.
6. Go home and rewrite.
7. Draft two!
8. Another informal reading or a rehearsal for a public reading.
    - Throughout this, I'll make changes based on what I hear.
9. Reading in front of an audience.
    - I like to find a spot in the back corner and watch both the actors and the audience.
        - When do the actors stumble?
        - When is the play slow?
        - When does the audience laugh?
        - Does the audience ever get restless?

- During this, I'm watching *and* taking millions of notes.
- Sometimes these end with a discussion, where I'll write down as much of what is said as I can.

10. Got home and rewrite.
11. Draft Three!
13. I'll send this draft far and wide to theaters and schools looking to work on new plays.

From there, my rewriting process is dependent in part on the development and/or production opportunities I can find for the script. How many drafts will I end up having of each new full-length? So far, as few as four, and as many as twenty-four. When do I put readings together with readers who aren't me? I like to plan a month or more out; this gives me a hard deadline on a new draft. After all, if people are moving their lives around to help me, I'd better be ready for them.

These days, I'll often try to find a project a home before I even begin the first draft, reaching out to see if any of my collaborators would be interested in commissioning me. Commissions are incredibly helpful as they come with support. Sometimes that support is development, sometimes it's money, sometimes it's a world premiere, sometimes it's publication, and sometimes, when you are very fortunate, it's all four. I'm the playwright in residence at the Egyptian YouTheatre, which has commissioned *Cheerleaders VS. Aliens*, *The Night Witches*, and *The Summer I Howled*. I also have a collaborator who teaches at the University of Utah and lets me bring in new work to read with her students pretty much whenever I have something I need to hear, and recently, she's commissioned a water polo play from me, *Hear Us Roar*. When working on a project with a home at a theater, you usually work out all of the development the play will need to get it ready for production and then publication.

I've also developed relationships with publishers like Stage Partners, who commissioned *The Book Women* and *The Hardy Girls* from me, both of which were published first, produced second. Both directions are exciting for me, as a writer. It means fewer of my plays will never see the light of day, and helps me focus on what theaters, schools, and publishers are looking for. All of my commissions have come from the bridges I've built and the community I've cultivated. I'll get into detail about community in a few chapters.

I know my process because I've done this more than a hundred times (remember, I have a bunch of plays folks don't see), and I have a ton of short plays and one-acts bouncing around. You learn about writing plays and your craft no matter the length of the play.

From building my craft I know that I need other people once I start to think the play is perfect. That's a sure sign to me that I need fresh eyes. It's taken me a lot of time, and a lot of pages, to figure out what I expect from each draft. To know when I need actors, or an audience, or designers, or a director. When I think a play is ready for production or publication. I've learned all of this from practice. From honing craft. And just like not all of my plays' journeys are the same, my rewriting craft and yours will probably differ. Part of the journey is learning what you need from each step of rewriting—learning what your first draft to world premiere looks like.

QUAGMIRE

QUAGMIRE. AS IN BOG. AS IN MUD. As in, dare I say it, writer's block. I get stuck, just as every writer, since writers started writing, gets stuck. We get stuck for lots of reasons: overwork, stress, lack of inspiration, lack of motivation, the list goes on and on. But how do you work yourself out of being stuck? That's the million-dollar question.

The key to knowing how to unstick yourself is knowing your writing instrument. You get to know your writer's instrument both by writing and also steering yourself through muddy times. Here are ways I get out of quagmires.

WRITING EVERY DAY, BRAIN DRAIN

I don't believe that a writer must write every day. However, when I feel lost and aimless, I'll turn back to daily **brain drains**. This draining of everyday worries, woes, and highlights clears my brain and gives space to think about writing. It has the added benefit of allowing you to practice writing without judgment. A giant source of writer's block for me comes from me not being satisfied with how my words are falling onto the page. The nature of the brain drain encourages us to allow anything to fall out onto the page, and taking judgment out of writing allows our instruments to relax. Which can help you get back in the grove and out of the mud.

Feel free to flip back to Act One of the book and refresh yourself on the brain drain, or just give yourself a timer and start writing. Experiment with giving yourself different amounts of time to see what's the most helpful. The brain drain combines organic writing with structure, the timer, and uses that structure to put pressure on your writer muscles to grow even in this muddy time.

WALKING AND/OR EXERCISING

I'll spend hours and days trying to get my characters to do what I want, and they just won't budge. I'll bang my hands and head on my keyboard, I'll scribble in my notebook, but nothing helps. Eventually, a little voice will pop up and tell me: "time to move," and I know there's nothing to it but a long walk. Writing is a non-physical activity, but humans need balance. And sometimes what our instrument needs more than anything is to move. What that movement is is dealer's choice, just something that gets you out of your brain and into your body.

I'd advise not to multitask with podcasts or audiobooks when you're trying to get unstuck. Part of the trick is that while you're trying to tire your body out, you want your brain to get a little bored. The combination of moving with boredom will cause your gears to turn and open up doors you wouldn't be able to access sitting at a desk. So as you sweat, let that mind wander. Look at the sky. Breathe fresh air. Get your heart pumping. Even if this doesn't break you out of the mud, you'll at least have had a pleasant time.

HOUSEWORK

I am so sorry. This, like the exercise prescribed above, must seem awfully rude of me. "Get over writer's block with exercise and folding laundry!" Brought to you by the Super-Secret Moms' Strategy Coalition.

But honestly, like exercise, it's a physical activity that doesn't involve a whole lot of thinking. Turn on some tunes and boogie while you soap up the dishes or toil in your garden. And again, as with exercising, let your mind wander. Trust me when I tell you that your brain will, in some deep dark corner, continue to work on whatever problem has slowed you down. I don't know why, but your brain knows what you're working on, even if you're not actively picking at it, and taking a break just might allow your brain to work it out.

BRAINSTORMING LISTS, BABY!

I know I've talked a lot about lists, and even more about **brainstorming**, but they're super helpful in my craft. I have two different modes: timed and quantity. With both I try to not think and just let the words happen. If it's a specific play problem I'm facing, I might brainstorm solutions and then write out more than one version before settling on what I'll try out next.

Brainstorming might not seem like much, but all writing is writing. Even if I never use it, even if it stays locked in a drawer or a file on my computer, having written something makes me a stronger and more focused writer in the long run.

PLAY WITH PROMPTS

Maybe you're stuck on figuring out the ending of your play, or you don't know how to pick things up after intermission, or you're dealing with one of the million other tricky moments that pop up. When I hit those walls, I'll put down what I'm working on for a day and try out a prompt. This prompt might be for something brand new and completely unrelated to your current project, or maybe this prompt is an exploration into the world of your current project. Either way, following the specifications of a prompt can allow your brain a break on the current problem, while you still get to stretch those creative writing muscles. Jump back to Act One of this book, where you'll find lots of writing exercises, or do an internet search. There are countless writing prompts out there—make sure to hold on to prompts that really get your gears moving.

SIT IN THE MUD, AS IN TAKE A BREAK

Counterintuitive, maybe, but sometimes we are stuck for a very good reason. As we build up those writing muscles, they can get sore and overworked, just like if we were training to run a marathon. Any serious workout regimen for the body has built-in rest days, and writing muscles aren't so different. Sometimes I need a day off. Sometimes it's a week. Sometimes it's a month. Often, I'll take off the entire summer. In my time off I usually do a lot of baking, I watch a lot of British murder-mystery TV, I take long naps, I take long walks, and I just let my brain take a vacation. You need to trust your instrument. It'll still be there on the other side of the break, and it may even be stronger than before.

Because getting stuck is part of the journey, getting unstuck is too. Take your next bout of writer's block as an opportunity to learn more about your craft. Try out one or more of these suggestions. What helps? What doesn't? Do these spark any ideas for something else for you to try? Experiment and, as always, *play.*

FEEDBACK

FEEDBACK MAKES OUR PLAYS and our instruments stronger. Until your play gets in front of another person, it relies entirely on your own brain to see if the timing is correct, if the plot makes sense, if the characters feel believable, among all the other elements. Our brains will often fill in gaps for us, making it difficult, if not impossible, to see our own work clearly. When an outsider gets their hands on your play, they are in a much better position to see and identify those gaps and ask questions about them. It can be uncomfortable, and make your stomach turn. If you're anything like me, sharing what I write feels like opening up my chest and letting folks take a look at my heart. It feels dangerous because my writing is an extension of me. I pour time, energy, hopes, dreams, sometimes even blood, sweat, and tears into my plays, and so when I get feedback, it feels like I'm getting feedback on both my work *and* me as a person. All of that to say: receiving feedback takes nerves of steel. So how is it possible to make feedback tolerable for us mere mortals? Structure, structure, structure! Using structure, just like with writing a play, can make the whole process manageable. And, as an added bonus, learning how to take and give feedback builds up muscles that make us stronger writers.

THE FUNCTION OF FEEDBACK

Feedback should always serve the play and the playwright. The best feedback shines a light on the gap between what the playwright *wants* the play to be, and what the play currently *is*. In the first draft of my play *The Night Witches*, I didn't realize until I heard it read out loud by a group of actors that one of the characters had only one line in the entire play. She literally entered, said hello to another character, and was then silently onstage for the rest of the play. Now, maybe that was intentional, maybe her almost total silence was imperative to the script. If folks are asking questions about it, the fact that it is imperative might not be made clear. The other possibility, which was the case in this instance, was that with a total of nine characters, I hadn't realized that one of them had only one line when I was writing it, and I didn't realize it when I read the whole play out loud to myself in my office either. My brain had filled that gap in for me, making it impossible for me to see.

Feedback allows you to experience your work through brand-new eyes. Eyes that haven't been staring at it and working on it for weeks, months, or years. These new eyes will see things that your eyes often won't register. These new eyes will discover things you didn't know were there, and probably miss things you were certain absolutely were.

We participate in the feedback process to further the development of someone's work. Everything said should be said in order to reach that end. How can we help this writer write the best version of the script that they are writing? Not the script that we're imagining it could be, but the script that the writer is actually writing. Which means that a lot of giving feedback is taking ourselves out of the equation completely and thinking about two major things:

- What is this play right now?
- What does the writer want this play to be?

THERE'S NOTHING WRONG WITH KEEPING THINGS POSITIVE

A common feedback trap is the idea that pointing out everything that we didn't like will benefit the writer and the work. This is almost never the case. It's important to remember that when we share work, it's like letting someone take a peek at our hearts. Writing is personal, and we shouldn't aim to make it otherwise. What we should aim for, instead, is to make our feedback as far from an attack as possible. That isn't to say that there's not room for critique—we'll get to that—but I think more important than critique is creating a positive environment for writers of all experience levels to share their work and not feel ashamed. To that end, I start with positive feedback first whether I'm giving feedback to another writer or having someone give feedback to me. I'll start by asking questions like:

- What popped off the page?
- What made you laugh?
- What made you cry?
- What made you lean in?

Sharing your work is hard; rewarding that brave act right out of the gate with "warm fuzzies" makes writers feel safer. And this isn't just to protect the writer. As we're sharing our heart, if we immediately get told all the ways our heart could be better, our brains will often stop listening in order to protect ourselves. Feedback that we don't hear can't be helpful feedback.

And there's plenty to learn from an entirely positive feedback session. If a room full of people are mentioning all of the moments in a play that left a lasting impression, and no one mentions the dream ballet from Act Two, that would lead me to go back to that section and try to work out why it had such little resonance.

NEUTRAL FEEDBACK

Neutrality isn't positive or negative, neutrality isn't an opinion, and neutrality certainly isn't "let me tell you how to write this play." I find neutral feedback helpful for two reasons: the first is that I think that after positive feedback, neutral feedback is the most conducive for developing anything artistic, and the second is that giving neutral feedback is hard, and figuring out how to do it well will make you a stronger writer.

I find that neutral questions are especially fruitful places to start. Questions are an act of curiousity, and truly neutral questions help get to the heart of how the play is functioning on the page in the moment, and if that is in line with what the writer actually wants from it. Neutral questions I might ask, include:

- What is the play? How would you describe the play?
- How is the play functioning?
- How is [insert element of the play] functioning?
- What reaction are you hoping to achieve from [insert element of the play]?

Both asking and answering neutral questions can be a great way to grow your analytical brain. Though, as a rule in my feedback sessions, writers don't ever have to answer a question they don't want to. For example, I almost never answer questions I am asked, neutral or otherwise, preferring to answer those questions in my rewrites instead of a group setting.

WHY OPINIONS AREN'T THAT IMPORTANT

Opinions are often the least helpful aspect when seeking or giving feedback. Maybe you were bit by a dog when you were three, and ever since, you've harbored great resentment toward all dog-kind, which makes you absolutely hate my dog opera. Your opinion is valid, but your opinion will not move my dog opera forward in the development process. Remember those two questions we asked before:

- What is this play now?
- What does the writer want the play to be?

Not liking dogs will not serve as feedback because it speaks to neither of these essential questions. I'm not saying that opinions can never be helpful, but if your opinion doesn't fit in with either of the questions above, it might just be something you write down for yourself and don't share with the writer.

And flipping this around, if you're getting feedback that's couched in an opinion and doesn't fit in at all with the two questions above, you are free to ignore it. That's one of the beautiful aspects of feedback: you can ignore any of the feedback you want. Keep what serves you as the writer, and your play.

GIVE IT STRUCTURE

Structure is helpful in plays themselves, but also in giving and receiving feedback. As I've said before, it's hard to show folks the heart beating inside your chest. You feel exposed. Having structure can alleviate some of that pressure, and it will make the feedback more direct. There are a few different modes of feedback that already exist too, so you don't have to figure out how to structure feedback on top of figuring out how to structure a play!

If you'd like a leg up on what to search for, I can't recommend Liz Lerman's Critical Response Process enough (https://lizlerman.com/critical-response-process/); it's strict structure puts the artist in the driver's seat. It is a four-step method that starts with statements of meaning, moves on to questions from the creating artist, then allows neutral questions from the audience, and ends with opinions, subject to permission from the creating artist. I will often combine steps from her process with elements from M. H. Abrams's critical response framework, which focuses on *what* the creation is and *how* it is currently functioning. I learned (and stole) this combination from Michelle Carter, one of my brilliant professors from grad school. Read both, try out both. Take what serves you, forget what doesn't.

ASK FOR WHAT YOU NEED

Feedback should always serve the play and the playwright. You should always feel empowered to ask for what you need in the feedback process. Maybe your brain hasn't fully digested hearing the dream ballet from Act Two out loud for the first time, and you know that you need to marinate on it longer before you get an outside take, or maybe you're itching to hear how the ending left folks feeling. If it's what you need, let it be known. Much like with working on letting your words flow freely onto the page, if your inner writer has an instinct with feedback, let that instinct be heard. Best news of all, you are still in charge of your play. It is still, and will always be, your play. And because of that, you are still in charge with what feedback you use, and what feedback you ignore.

So think it over, ask away, take what serves you, and ignore what doesn't.

UNIVERSAL FEEDBACK

If you're lucky enough to be a part of a writers' group, or in a classroom setting that reads multiple writers' works, I encourage you to write down everything said in those sessions. Another of my brilliant teachers from grad school, Brian Thorstenson, would tell us before we shared and received feedback during our workshop, "Even if we're not talking about *your* play, we're talking about *your* play." That might feel a little bit like a riddle, but what he meant was that there is often a universality to feedback. If everyone in the group or class wonders what the protagonist wants when we read the work of the playwright who sits next to me, that makes me wonder if what *my* protagonist wants is clear enough. Questions about pace, character, genre, or any other element of someone else's play, are questions that can always be applied to more than one work. I took Brian's advice and wrote everything down, saving questions to ask them of myself later. It's a very waste-not-want-not mentality that both serves the development of projects and the development of craft. Also, if we think back to that heart we're showing others, it can often be easier to hear feedback and questions aimed at someone else's heart, instead of our own. Yes, they're not specifically talking about your play . . . but also, aren't they kinda still talking about your play?

HOW I INCORPORATE FEEDBACK

Now that we know all the different types of feedback, how do you know what to listen to? How do you know what to ignore? The answer to that, my friends, comes back again to craft. It is through the development of your craft that you will learn your answers to those questions.

For me, knowing what my play *is* and what I want it *to be* helps me navigate feedback. It's like music: the more you know the song you're playing, the more you know when a note rings false. For example, say I'm getting feedback on my dog opera and one of my readers asks a neutral question about what choices led me to not have any cat characters. Now, if I know what I want out of this dog opera, I might know that it has to be a 100 percent dogs-only cast; they're barking the whole time after all—how would a cat ever understand that? I may wonder if I didn't explain the rules of the world well enough, or what they think a cat character could offer that the opera is missing. If I'm not excited about feedback, I'm happy to throw it away. Remember, it's all about the playwright. Feedback givers shouldn't ever make it about themselves. If they want a cat so badly, they can write their own animal opera. But, on the other hand, maybe I hear that question and I think, wow, why *aren't* there any cat characters? Could I rewrite the antagonist as a giant orange tomcat? When I get feedback that sets my imagination running, I know it's a keeper.

And that's all craft. Intuition. Being willing to explore another person's idea, and seeing if it fits or belongs in your work. The more you know your play, your springboard, your genre, your time and place, your characters, and your structure, the more you will sense what feedback builds up your play stronger, and what feedback doesn't serve you. This comes with practice, patience, and fortitude. You will most likely need to listen to a lot of feedback before you know what you should and shouldn't listen to.

When I was first starting out, nearly all feedback felt like a personal attack. I knew I needed it. I knew it made my work and my craft stronger, but it didn't make it any easier. One trick I learned was to write everything down in the moment. All the thoughts, all the questions, all the opinions, but really if you don't write down all the opinions, that's probably fine . . . And then I'd go home and give it a day. Or a week. And come back to what I'd noted down when I was alone and in the safety of my office. It's a lot easier to be neutral with others' feedback when you give yourself time and space. Another of my rules from early on was that I would never answer a question I didn't want to. Will I write it down? Will I think about it? You betcha. But this feedback is about the writer. I wouldn't answer the question in the room, and I often still won't, but I do try and answer those questions in my rewrite. That's what matters. That's where it counts.

Feedback is essential for rewriting and developing plays. Learning about how to take and give feedback is a lifelong lesson for everyone who wants to participate in the arts. Much like your muscles for writing, feedback muscles need building as well, both in the bravery required in sharing your work (and the willingness you need to hear the responses) and in giving feedback. After all, once you get better at giving others feedback, you can use those skills on your own work any time you want.

COMMUNITY

THEATRE IS ALL ABOUT PEOPLE. Not only does our writing reflect people, but we also collaborate with a lot of people through new play development, and end up putting a show up in front of (hopefully) a whole lot of people. Building a playwriting and theatre **community** is essential. Not only because it's who will help and support your work, just as you will help and support theirs, but also because sometimes you need a late-night milkshake and vent session, and that's significantly less awkward if you have someone to do it with.

But how do you find and/or build a community? It takes work, but it is essential. Here are a few things to try to get you started.

GO SEE SHOWS!

Go see as many productions as possible. It will both give you a taste for what your local theatre community is interested in and introduce you to a ton of artists. If you see a show and you love the lighting design, email the lighting designer and let them know you were impressed by their work. Same goes for the other designers, director, and the actors! Feel free to hang around after the show and tell them face-to-face too. Did you wonder before where to find all those actors who'll read drafts out loud for you? Local productions are a great place to start.

If your budget doesn't allow for regular ticket purchasing, know that volunteers can often earn tickets for plays. Ushers get to watch the show as they work, or you can become a reader.

Many theaters use volunteer readers as first-round reviewers for incoming scripts. These readers write reports of the plays they read for the literary staff, which identify any potential good fits for their programming. When I lived in the Bay Area, I was a reader for Berkeley Repertory Theatre, which helped me build my analytical skills, and gave me a free pair of tickets for every six plays I read and wrote a report on. Reach out to theaters and see what they need. Most of the time, they'll be jumping at the opportunity to get more help.

FINDING YOUR THEATRE COMMUNITY

Are you in school? Studying theatre? If so, you're in a prime position to be surrounded by actors, directors, and designers. Grab an empty classroom and some of your peers and hold impromptu readings of whatever you're working on. When you leave school, you will most likely never have it so easy as far as proximity to free space and eager participants, so take advantage while you can.

Out of school? Investigate if there's a playwright group in your area, or an online Zoom group you could join. These all have different structures: sometimes they're open to anyone, and sometimes you need to apply or be invited. The meetings themselves vary quite a lot; you might hear a whole full-length play from a single playwright, hear ten pages from different playwrights' works, or there might be another setup entirely. If it's a group that invites local actors to come and read, you'll have the added benefit of connecting with them as well! Do some research and see where you might be able to fit in, and if there isn't anything that fits, start your own group!

Building a community in theatre is essential for the long-term theatre artist. It gives you a web of support, as well as a group of people with a vested interest in growing your artistry because you have a vested interest in growing theirs. Plays can't be done with a single person—we need, at the very least, an audience to watch. More often than not, we need producers, directors, designers, and actors. Find out who you want in your community, support them, and they may just turn around and support you in return.

READING

WHEN I WAS STUDYING to be an actor with Coach, he told us that all aspiring actors should be **reading** one play a week. How else can you know what to audition for, or what playwrights you're the most excited about? If you're not sure what work is out there, you can't make informed decisions on where you fit. It's excellent advice for an aspiring actor, and it's excellent advice for an aspiring playwright.

You don't, and shouldn't, limit your reading to plays alone. Plays, of course, are important in your reading diet, but there's lots more under the sun. You never know what nugget will inspire your next piece, or what story will sit dormant in your brain for years only to become essential in some faraway project down the line.

One play/novel/poetry collection a week may feel like too much for you, and that's fine. It's all about finding out what works for you. It's another step in discovering exactly what your instrument needs to stay in tune and perform its best. And while I don't always agree with "writers should write every day," I am a huge believer in "reading makes you a better writer." Doesn't matter the genre or form. Find out what your instrument needs and read, read, read!

USE THE LIBRARY

I borrow a lot from my library. Both in person, and through an app with audiobooks (I love a good audiobook). If your library is like mine, it might be lacking in the dramatic texts department, especially with anything written within the last twenty years. But it should be a big help in many other forms: periodicals, fiction, non-fiction, poetry, and others. Read every book from your favorite author, read books by folks you've never heard of, read media you've never experienced, as well as forms you know you love. All of it will influence and grow your instrument.

THE NEW PLAY EXCHANGE

Have you signed up for the New Play Exchange yet (https://newplayexchange.org/)? Because you really should sign up for the New Play Exchange. The New Play Exchange is an amazing tool, and worth every penny. Playwrights can upload their scripts to the database for fellow playwrights, theaters, directors, teachers, or anyone really, to find. If you're looking for the most economical place to get access to the largest amount of new work, look no further. There is a huge range of plays on the site, and you're encouraged to leave positive reviews when you read or see something you love. I would encourage you to respond to how the play is functioning in your notebook first, before you post anything, as it builds that analytical muscle we've been talking about. And don't worry about finding the "best" or "strongest" scripts. You can learn about writing plays by reading any level of work. But a good trick I use to find plays I connect with is first finding a playwright I enjoy, and then see what they're reading and recommending. Usually that'll set me down a lovely rabbit hole of fresh and exciting new work.

FIND FREE PLAYS ONLINE

Explore play publishers' websites to see if any of their scripts are available to read online. Different publishers have different setups worth looking into. For example, Stage Partners (https://www.yourstagepartners.com/) makes every play in their catalogue available to read online for free if you simply create an account on their site.

OBJECTIVE (Yes! Again!)

I DID WARN YOU that **objectives** are important, and I wasn't lying. Way back in Act One, we learned that everybody everywhere has an objective all the time, that not one interaction goes by where we don't want something. And it's true. Which is why objective is the only tool that gets double coverage. But this time, instead of what our characters want, I want to know:

What do YOU want?

What do YOU want as a WRITER?

What do YOU want for your WRITING?

These are big questions, questions that you will have to ask yourself over and over again. Because, just like our characters, if we don't identify what we want, it's hard to take action to get there. Do you see your plays being produced on Broadway? Internationally? At regional theaters? At dinner theaters? High schools? Colleges? Get specific! Think about where you want to see your work. There are no wrong answers. Nothing too big, nothing too small. Think about exactly where you want your plays produced. Specifically know which publishers you want to publish your work and what artists you want to work with. In my writing, my goals differ for each play, but all of it serves my overarching goal, kind of like a macro-objective for an entire play versus one of the micro-objectives in a scene.

To figure this out, you'll need to see a lot of theatre. It also involves a whole lot of reading. In seeing and reading other work, and following other playwrights' careers, you can make a basic map for yourself. It will also help when you start submitting your plays, because applications often want an artistic statement, which is your objective as a writer! Once you've got a lot of reading and watching under your belt, you can start to recognize what's missing in the theatre scene. What should be there but isn't? Once you identify that, and identify your own writing objectives, find the overlap, and that's where you should set your sail. After all, if you're interested in something and there's a lack of it in the field, then you are very much needed. Your voice. You.

So what do you want? As the Spice Girls said, "Tell me what you want, what you really, really want." Shout it to the world. Or scribble it down in your trusty sidekick of a notebook, and then start heading in that direction. Let's, for the final time, get a timer ready. Twenty minutes, or maybe more. Write down what you want. Where do you see your career in five years, ten years, twenty? No one will see this, so don't let embarrassment slow you down. Maybe you'll even write something down that surprises you. Repeat this exercise every year or so. Every time you're not sure what you are doing.

Got all that? Timer ready? GO!

Curtain Call

You did it! Not only do you have a toolbox filled with tools to develop your work, you also have tools to develop your craft, and a draft of a play! Congratulations! Writing is hard; coming this far should be celebrated. Take the time to celebrate! Go on your favorite hike, or give yourself that play anthology collection you've been eyeing, or go to see a brand-new piece of theatre! Something that feels special to you. Remember: just like it's an important skill to learn how to let the words fall out onto the page without judgment, it's also important to learn how to celebrate wins. But before you leave to celebrate your victory, I'd like to leave you with one last final scene from our backstage *Romeo and Juliet* adventure:

(The greenroom. After the curtain call on opening night, we hear the applause petering out. JULIET and ROMEO enter with a flurry of energy.)

JULIET: Wow wow wow. I mean, WOW!

ROMEO: Sounds like we've got another convert.

JULIET: I wouldn't go that far—

ROMEO: And may I quote, "Wow wow wow. I mean, WOW!" You wanted to quit just a few short weeks ago! And now here you are basking in the glory of opening night!

JULIET: Opening night is pretty wonderful, I will admit that.

ROMEO: You love it, 'fess up.

JULIET: Love is a big word. It was terrifying. And maybe also exciting, at times. All those applause and people, kind of a mix of both.

ROMEO: I get that.

JULIET: But also, I don't know, I've never done anything like this before and I made it through! I am a lead in a Shakespeare play! And I survived my first performance in front of an audience!

(ROMEO applauds JULIET.)

ROMEO: And you did it with style!

JULIET: It did help that there was a murder to solve. I'm not sure I would have found the courage to stay without that mystery thrown in.

ROMEO: You would have stayed, acting was under your skin after auditions. I'm not saying it wouldn't have been hard, or that the murder wasn't a welcome distraction for you, but I think you would have stuck it out no matter what. And now you've done it!

JULIET: And now I've done it! And put that murderous Assistant Stage Manager, who murdered the former Assistant Stage Manager, behind bars, as they deserve!

ROMEO: Here, here! So what's next? Have you seen the audition sign-up sheet for the next production?

JULIET: I did see, I've decided I'm going to read the script first this time. Curious if there's a tree in this one.

ROMEO: Always with the tree!

JULIET: I just want to finish what I set out to do, you know?

ROMEO: Not at all . . . So, the cast and crew usually all goes out together opening night, it's kinda tradition. In fact they've probably started without us, we should get a move on!

JULIET: How can they be so quick? Don't they have to change?

ROMEO: Tradition also dictates that they go out in costume.

JULIET: Oh, I'll bet Costumes just loves that!

ROMEO: Good thing we have you around, in case they get any murderous ideas in their head!

JULIET: Indeed!

ROMEO: Can I give you a ride? To the party? And, I don't know, maybe you're tired, but maybe we could just make an appearance and then head off to do our own thing? Just, you know, the two of us?

JULIET: Are you, Romeo, asking out me, Juliet?

ROMEO: I guess I kind of am.

JULIET: Lead on, good Romeo, lead on.

(They exit together. End.)

Acknowledgments

I'd like to take a moment to thank all the lovely people who helped me to write an actual book! Many thanks to my family! Alex, my wonderful partner and husband, who constantly reminded me to eat and made delicious things to feed me. My amazing Viking children, Audrey and Jonah, who always forgive me when I, yet again, am late to pick them up because I was lost writing. My mom, who always believed I could do anything. My dad, who expanded my world through so many amazing books. My siblings: my sister Anna for buying me all those journals growing up, my sister Kelly for always playing pretend with her obnoxious younger sister, and my brother Oliver, who was always ready to be read or told stories to. And my incredibly supportive family in-law: Katy, Art, and Thomas. I'd also like to thank a few dear friends: Jessi, Chris, Liz, Claire, Danielle, Kat, Ashley, Jamie, and Andra. You all make my life better just by being a part of it.

I would also like to thank from the very bottom of my heart all of the educators that I've had over the years, both in and out of official institutes, who pushed me to be the best me I could be. Specifically, thank you Juan Castro, Kris Clark, Michelle Carter, Brian Thorstenson, Roy Conboy, Peter Sinn Nachtrieb, Rhonnie Washington, George Ye, Dr. Ogden, Megan Cohen, Heather Helinksy, Martine Kei Green-Rogers, Lauren Gunderson, Kenneth Jones, and E. M. Lewis.

Finally, a huge thank you to everyone at Stage Partners, but most especially Maria Pizzarello who guided me through the process of writing an entire book.

About the Author

RACHEL BUBLITZ is an award-winning and internationally produced playwright known for telling stories about women and creating exciting new work for young performers. She has received a Rolling World Premiere with the National New Play Network, and is currently the resident playwright of the Egyptian YouTheatre in Park City, Utah. Her plays include: *Ripped* (produced by Z Space and Good Company Theatre), *The Night Witches* (commissioned by Egyptian YouTheatre, with over fifty productions worldwide), *Burst* (produced by Alleyway Theatre), *The Summer I Howled* (commissioned and developed with Egyptian YouTheatre), and many more. Awards include: Will Glickman Award for Best Bay Area Premiere (*Ripped*), Shubert Fendrich Memorial Playwriting Contest (*Cheerleaders VS. Aliens*), and PlayGround's June Anne Baker Prize (*Reading Babar in 2070*). She has just over a dozen titles with Stage Partners: *The Book Women, The Hardy Girls, Of Serpents and Sea Spray, The Red House Monster, Midnight Bandits* (included in *Rogues' Gallery*), *I Said Run.* (included in *It's Her Say*), and *Holly, Jolly, and Extra Folly,* a collection of ten-minute holiday plays all by Rachel. In addition to her work with Stage Partners, she's published with Dramatic Publishing (*The Night Witches* and *Burst*), Playscripts (*Biz Town, Ghost House,* and *Operation Chicken Takeover*), Pioneer Drama Service (*Cheerleaders VS. Aliens*), YouthPLAYS (*The Summer I Howled, The Elves,* and *No Talking Allowed!*), and others. She is a member of the Dramatists Guild of America and has an MFA from San Francisco State University. When she isn't writing, she's mostly watching her daughter dominate at water polo or gardening with her son.

About Stage Partners

Stage Partners is an independent play publisher dedicated to making exceptional plays accessible to all theatres and schools. Founded in 2015 by two playwrights with extensive backgrounds in theatrical publishing and licensing, Stage Partners was created with the simple idea that regardless of whether you are a new drama teacher or an experienced artistic director, finding the perfect new play should be easy, engaging, and exciting. With scripts that are always free to read, lightning-fast licensing, production & educational resources, and a passionate staff, Stage Partners is committed to offering industry-best services to both its customers and its playwrights. If you are looking for a publishing partner that understands that making theatre happen is hard work, but discovering a great new play should be a breeze, join us at www.yourstagepartners.com and we'll begin together.

www.ingramcontent.com/pod-product-compliance
Ingram Content Group UK Ltd.
Pitfield, Milton Keynes, MK11 3LW, UK
UKHW021704190726
13853UKWH00001B/416

9 798890 992604